THE PROSPERING POWER OF LOVE

Catherine Ponder

Published by
DEVORSS & COMPANY
P.O. Box 550, Marina del Rey, CA 90294

CONTENTS

reach the aloof, intellectual type. *Fourth*: How to reach the zealous, quarrelsome type. *Fifth:* How to reach the fearful body devotees. *Sixth*: How to reach the loving-works type. *Seventh*: How to reach the unstable wanderers. Write to your own angel. Angel-writing produces neither hurt nor harm

Love dissolves debt for a businessman. Lawyer uses love to collect money. How they used love to prosper. Divine love can meet every need. Love is released through the prosperous tenth. The secret of financial increase. The countless blessings of tithing. A final way for invoking the prospering power of love.

INTRODUCTION...

THE MULTI-FACETED POWER OF LOVE

A Special Message From The Author

Much of the material in this book was first published as a series of articles in the early 1960's. I shall always be grateful to the late James A. Decker, my long-time editor, for putting the material together and titling it for its publication in 1966 by Unity Books. Since that time it has been one of my most popular books.

The early reports I received from those studying this book included that of a businesswoman

in Kansas City, Missouri, who told me she was
healed of a painful back condition as she
learned to daily call on divine love.

Another early report was that from a busi-
nesswomen's group in Michigan who decided to
spend some time at their meetings affirming
divine love for the club and its members.

Within a short time, several of those middle-
aged women got married! One career woman
had been widowed for twenty-five years. Yet
she soon went off to Southern California to live
with her new husband in a beautiful home near
the ocean.

As for the club—so many women in that
group got married that they had to reorganize
the whole club!

I am grateful to the officials of Unity School
for allowing me to now update much of the original book published in 1966 and to have it re-
published by my California publisher, so that it
may reach an ever-growing readership.

HAPPINESS REPORTS

Of all of the self-help books I have written in
the past several decades, *The Prospering Power
of Love* is the one I have most often recommended: *first*, to those people who are beginning their inspirational search; *second*, to those
people with human relations problems, which
most people experience on occasion as a part of

their growth into greater understanding; and *third*, to those people who are looking for a book containing a simple, yet inspirational approach that they can share with others as a means of help.

The reports I have received from my readers over the years on love's prospering power have been multifaceted:

Past Due Accounts Are Paid In Alabama: I have been working on the collection of past due accounts by using the ideas from *The Prospering Power of Love*. The first results came last night when a young man brought me five $100 bills!

From A Mental Hospital To A New Life In New York: My mother gave me *The Prospering Power of Love* at a time when I was in a mental hospital. I had gone through many tribulations: divorce, a missing child, and paralysis, to name a few. One minister said I had experienced more in thirty years than most people had experienced at age ninety.

I am now out of the hospital and employed. I have my child with me, and I can walk again after the paralysis. We are living nicely and planning to buy a home. I have been told by doctors that I am one of the strongest people they have ever met. I am optimistic about my future as I continue to study my worn, coffee-stained copy of that book. We have come a long way together!

Taking Charge After Depression and Pain In The Deep South: I gave a tenant, who had gotten behind in her rent payments, a copy of *The Prospering Power of Love*. Since she was financially desperate, she was receptive to that book. She was also deeply touched that anyone cared what happened to her. So she began to declare that divine love was at work in her life.

She had been in constant pain and was bleeding. Surgery had been recommended as the only cure. As she began to call on Divine Love to help her, the pain and bleeding stopped. The depression lifted, she began making business decisions again, and even went on a diet to lose weight.

Thanks to the power of divine love, she is beginning to take charge of her life, rather than continuing to feel that she is the helpless victim of circumstances. I rejoice that the miracle of love is at work, and I marvel at the changes that are taking place within and around her.

Romance Comes To A Senior Citizen In England: I have been studying *The Prospering Power of Love*, and out of the blue, love has come in the form of a gentleman of my age (72 years). He is a widower and financially comfortable. It is his companionship that is so wonderful. I shall always bless that book for the happiness its study has brought into my life.

HOW THESE IDEAS HELPED THE AUTHOR

I am grateful for the way the prospering power of love has expanded my understanding and life since I first wrote about it. Much of the original material in this book was written in the early 1960's while I was living in an apartment overlooking the University of Texas in Austin, where my husband taught. We had recently married and that was an especially happy time for me. However, before my articles on the subject had been published in book form, my husband had passed on suddenly and unexpectedly. Love no longer seemed so much a many-splendored thing as a many-splintered one.

"First comes illumination, then comes initiation, after which comes the harvest of new good," wrote the mystics of old. I had earlier learned and written about the power of divine love. That had been a period of illumination about love for me. Now, perhaps, I was receiving a deeper initiation in love in my own life.

During much of the rest of that decade I had an opportunity to live with the ideas found in this book. They were a comfort, a companion, and a guide to me. During that period, I wrote chapters on divine love in several other books.[1] It was also during that decade that I began to lecture extensively all over the United States. A copy of *The Prospering Power of Love* usually accompanied me on those trips into the heat or cold, on long flights, in strange cities, and while working with new people in unfamiliar surroundings.

---

1. See *The Dynamic Laws of Prosperity, The Healing Secret of the Ages, Open Your Mind to Prosperity* and *The Dynamic Laws of Healing*.

But the inworking is always followed by the outworking. In 1970 happy changes came in my life which led to a move to San Antonio, Texas. This was another especially memorable period since it was there that I soon remarried and my husband provided me with my first home. A few years later we made a move I had long thought about, to Palm Desert, California, where I continued with my by-now global work. We settled in an old movie colony neighborhood filled with tropical beauty. There I began to write a series of new books, and, at my husband's insistence, to lead a more normal and balanced way of life than I had known before.

Further expansion has come gradually in my work and lifestyle in the years that have followed; and I trust there will be greater progress in the future. However, I find that regardless of my life circumstances — bitter or sweet, meager or comfortable — the ideas contained in these pages continue to apply.

Over the years when people have described every conceivable type of problem to me, I have often found myself suggesting that they study *The Prospering Power of Love*.

Why?

Because as Ghandi once said, "Throughout history, the way of love and truth has always won."

THE AUTHOR'S INVITATION

A Missouri businessman recently wrote:

> I was drawn into the Truth Movement many
> years ago through *The Prospering Power of
> Love*. I have studied it often and given away
> more copies than I can remember. When I
> started applying the ideas it contained, first I
> changed. Then my life changed. I am happy
> to report that my life has vastly improved over
> the years.

As for what to do with the ideas you find and
apply from this book, a California businessman
made this suggestion:

> Here is a statement that has meant a great
> deal to me over the years: "Love wasn't put in
> your heart to stay. Love isn't love until you give
> it away."

Since divine love is a prospering, enlightening, harmonizing, healing power, I trust that
your study of this book will bless your life in
many ways. As it does so, I invite you to write
and share with me the unfoldment of your own
unique "love story."

Catherine Ponder

P.O. Drawer 1278
Palm Desert, California 92261
U.S.A.

THE MIRACLE OF LOVE

— Chapter 1 —

Several years ago a businessman pointed out to me the success power of love. At the time, I was writing a series of prosperity articles. Hearing of my project, this stockbroker asked, "What do you have in your series about love?" Startled, I replied: "About love? This series is on prosperity." "I know," he said. "But it won't be complete without an article on the prosperity law of love and good will. Love is the greatest success power there is."

Then he told me how he had developed his own private success formula for "straightening out" troublesome people. He stated that when he became quiet and blessed them with an affirmation on love, it was as though an electric force was generated, to which they became attuned. Usually they responded quickly with harmonious attitudes and behavior. If not, further affirmations on love invariably produced harmonious results.

In recent times, we have heard much about the success power of love. A noted psychiatrist has stated that the greatest human need is the need for love, and that none of us can survive without it. Man must have love in his life in some form or he will perish. Love is the greatest power on earth, he states.

There is nothing new about these ideas on the power of love. It was the Master Psychologist of the ages who informed the lawyer that love was the greatest of all the commandments. Paul, one of the world's great intellectuals and a builder of early Christianity, also ascribed all power to love.

You are probably familiar with Henry Drummond's famous essay on love, in which he writes about Paul's epistle to the Corinthians (I Corinthians 13). In his essay, Drummond describes love as "the supreme gift," "the supreme good." He says,

> The final test of religion . . . is not religiousness, but love. . . . You will find as you look back upon your life that the moments that

stand out, the moments when you have really
lived, are the moments when you have done
things in a spirit of love.

Drummond then describes the various as-
pects of love in Paul's epistle as patience, kindness, generosity, humility, courtesy, unselfish-
ness, good temper, guilelessness, and sincerity.
He tells of how *a man read Paul's writings on
love once a week for three months, and how this
changed his whole life.*

PERSONAL AND IMPERSONAL LOVE

You and I might think of love in the terms
Paul uses to describe it. We can express these
qualities both as personal love and as impersonal love. Personal love could be expressed
as kindness, tenderness, courtesy, affection, approval, consideration, appreciation, devotion to
those in our family groups. Impersonal love is
basically the ability to get along with people,
without personal attachment or emotional in-
volvement. "I LOVE ALL PEOPLE AND ALL PEOPLE
LOVE ME, WITHOUT ATTACHMENT" is a fine statement to use often in developing a consciousness
of impersonal love and good will toward our
business associates and toward those with whom
we interact in our workaday world.

LOVE SOLVES BOTH PERSONAL
AND BUSINESS PROBLEMS

I know of a group of persons who once experimented with the power of love in a prayer group and found it to be the greatest thing in the world to solve both personal and business problems. Once a week these persons met for an hour and affirmed statements of divine love. They brought to these meetings their private prayer lists of people and situations they wished to bless with the success power of love. No one else saw their prayer lists, nor did they talk about the people and problems their prayer lists represented.

Instead, they quietly placed their hands on their individual prayer lists while they affirmed together various statements on divine love. "DIVINE LOVE IS DOING ITS PERFECT WORK IN ME AND THROUGH ME NOW" they affirmed for themselves, for their own health, wealth, and happiness; "DIVINE LOVE IS DOING ITS PERFECT WORK IN YOU AND THROUGH YOU NOW" they affirmed for those on their prayer lists.

For a number of weeks they met and affirmed statements of love over and over. In a quiet way, amazing things began to happen to the various members of that group and to the people for whom they prayed. One businesswoman was out of harmony with a number of her friends. As she began dwelling on affirmations of love, her friends began appearing unexpectedly at the prayer group meetings, and reconciliation quickly took place.

Another businesswoman had been troubled for some time because of a misunderstanding that had arisen months previously between her and some friends. She had made every effort to apologize and bring about harmony and understanding again, but she had been coldly rebuffed in spite of her letters, telephone calls, and personal contacts.

One night during the regular prayer time as the group was affirming divine love for the names on the prayer lists, this woman and one other woman in the group both heard a popping noise in the air. The other woman discounted it, thinking it to be only her imagination. But after the meeting had concluded, the businesswoman came to her and confidentially said: "Did you hear that popping sound in the air? That wasn't your imagination: it really happened! That was the hard thoughts that have existed between me and my friends. I'm convinced that tonight, through our spoken words, divine love dissolved the hard thoughts and the inharmony that have existed between us. That was the dissolving power of love that you heard healing that situation!"

From that night on she had a completely different feeling about the situation. She felt peaceful and harmonious. She quietly gave thanks that divine understanding had been established and that divine love had helped the previous misunderstanding and hostility.

Some weeks later, though no outer change had come, she felt led to contact her friends again. This time, instead of rebuffing her, they reacted as though nothing had ever been wrong between them. The previous cordiality, understanding, and friendship were reestablished and continue even now.

LOVE IS WITHIN YOU

Perhaps you do not have access to such a prayer group. But you can still experience the success power of love. You have all the love you need for healing, prosperity, and happy human relationships right *within* yourself. Divine love is one of your mental and spiritual faculties. *You do not have to search outside yourself for love. You can begin releasing it from within outward, through your thoughts, words, actions, and affirmative prayers.* As you do, you will experience the success power of love in all its fullness as it works through people, situations, and conditions that concern you.

A world-renowned sociologist once conducted research studies at Harvard University on the power of love. Under his direction, a staff of scientists studied the subject of love. Their findings were that *love, like other good things, can be produced deliberately by human beings.* They stated that there is no reason why we cannot learn to generate love as we do other natural forces.

Thus there is no reason for you to feel disillusioned or disappointed if love has seemingly let you down or passed you by. Those who bitterly declare that their lives are without love are mistakenly looking to someone or something outside themselves for love. Begin realizing now that love is first *within* you and can be released through your thoughts, feelings, words, and actions. As you begin developing love from within outward, you are truly proving your method to be spiritual, scientific, and satisfying. You no longer feel at the mercy of people, situations, and conditions. You become master of your world and free from hurt, fear, disappointment, and disillusionment.

It is like developing an electric force. Love will begin to radiate outwardly into every part of your world, to attract to you the right people, situations, and conditions that will add to your success and happiness. You will soon realize that instead of your being at the mercy of the world, the world responds to your own thoughts and feelings; and that when your thoughts and feelings generate love, the world about you will happily respond in a most wonderful way! This is the success power of love.

THE SUCCESS POWER OF LOVE
HEALS MARRIAGE PROBLEMS

Many people are discovering this power in all departments of life. In the realm of human relationships it is all-powerful. A housewife told of having quarreled with her husband, after which he stormed out of the house. Having learned that she could generate love from within outward, she decided to try it in this marital crisis. Quietly she began to say over and over: "I CALL ON DIVINE LOVE TO HEAL OUR MARRIAGE NOW. I CALL ON DIVINE LOVE TO STRAIGHTEN OUT AND ADJUST THIS SITUATION."

In a little while a sense of peace overwhelmed her, and she busily began preparing dinner for her husband in the faith that he would return to enjoy it. (After previous quarrels, it had not always been so.) Soon she heard the door open, and her husband entered, in a happy frame of mind, carrying a box of candy for her. Their quarrels became fewer and less severe, and in due time their marriage was entirely healed of inharmony.

A businesswoman related a similar experience concerning the power of love in her marriage, which had been unhappy for some time. There had been many quarrels—much bickering, tension, inharmony. One night when there had been a prolonged and bitter quarrel, the woman thought: "We cannot go on. This inharmony is affecting our health, our business success, and our marriage. There must be a way out."

She began looking for something to read that might give her a sense of peace and hope, and she found these words: "LOVE MELTS SITUATIONS THAT SEEM IMPOSSIBLE," Over and over she said: "YES, IT IS TRUE. LOVE MELTS SITUATIONS THAT SEEM IMPOSSIBLE."

Formerly, reconciliation had come slowly and painstakingly after each quarrel. But as she continued dwelling on this statement of love, the inharmony and misunderstanding faded almost at once. That proved to be this couple's last bitter quarrel. Since that time, whenever inharmony has seemed near, she has quickly affirmed, "LOVE MELTS SITUATIONS THAT SEEM IMPOSSIBLE"; always this has cleared the air and harmony has been reestablished.

THE AUTHOR'S EXPERIENCES WITH
LOVE IN FAMILY MATTERS

Do you doubt that your thoughts and words of divine love can have equal power in your own life and affairs? I once had a simple family experience that convinced me that our thoughts of love do reach others more quickly and completely than we sometimes realize. One warm spring day I was in my study, trying to finish an article on love, when my teenage son came in. He had been playing golf all day, and was hungry and anxious to get home.

When I explained that I was trying to complete an article and would finish in a few minutes, he quietly left. Soon I thought I heard the study door open again, but since things at once became quiet, I did not turn to investigate. Some minutes later, when I had completed my work, I realized that my son had quietly returned and placed two red roses on my desk from the nearby rose garden. Without a word he had then left, to wait patiently for me. He had not known I was working on an article on love. Never before had he brought me flowers, but at that moment he seemed attuned to the very ideas I was dwelling on in the article, and he lovingly responded.

On still another occasion, he demonstrated to me the success power of love. One morning he left for school in an unhappy mood. All day I remembered it and felt badly that he had begun the day in such a state of mind. I felt that there was something I should have done or said to turn the tide of his thinking in the morning. All day as I remembered this incident I kept affirming, "DIVINE LOVE IS DOING ITS PERFECT WORK IN THIS SITUATION NOW."

That afternoon when he arrived home from school, he came into the house, put aside his books, and greeted me with the words, "Hi, beautiful!" I cannot remember when he had greeted me in such a manner before, but truly, love had done its perfect work that day!

THE MISSION OF LOVE

When you are inclined to wonder how thoughts and words of love can do much good in resolving various problems, remind yourself that loving words and loving thoughts seem supercharged with power to produce good. Indeed, it is the mission of love, both personally and impersonally, to produce eternal good in your life. Your part is not to wonder how love works, but just to dare to begin releasing it, from *within* yourself. When you do, you will always witness interesting and satisfying results.

LOVE CAN PROMOTE HEALTH

A doctor once showed me a medical book on psychosomatic illness. In this book a group of physicians had compiled their analyses of various illnesses and of the mental and emotional attitudes they felt caused these illnesses. I was amazed to see that in every analysis the need for love was listed.

For instance, in the case of stomach disorders of all types, one of the psychosomatic reasons given for such illness was "love needed." In the case of heart disorders, one of the reasons listed was "love needed."

In the case of skin disorders, one of the reasons listed was "need for approval," which is a form of love. (A bookkeeper stated that while experiencing a skin disorder she began a daily practice of placing her hands on her face and affirming, "DIVINE LOVE IS HEALING YOU NOW," and the skin disorder soon faded.)

In the case of female disorders, one of the reasons listed was "need for love." In the case of chronic fatigue, one of the psychosomatic reasons listed was "depression, insecurity, and need for love."

In the case of the common headache and migraine, one of the reasons listed was "insecurity and need for love." In the case of excessive weight and overeating, one of the reasons listed was "a feeling of dissatisfaction with life and a need for love." In the case of alcoholism and other excesses, one of the reasons listed was "feelings of inferiority and need for love."

The wonderful thing to remember is that when there is a need for love, we can begin supplying it from *within* ourselves. A businessman told me that he was healed of a painful condition of long standing after he began releasing love from within himself, by speaking words of love to his body. He had tried various treatments to no avail, and then he heard of the healing power of love. He began placing his hand on the painful area of his body, saying over and over, "I LOVE YOU." The pain subsided, and gradually faded away.

Cancer has been described as an "anxiety disease." The emotional histories of a large percentage of those who have cancer show that in some period of their lives they felt anxious, insecure or unloved, and that they subconsciously retained that feeling, which had often turned to bitterness, a critical state of mind, and may have even generated hostility and hate.

One authority has stated that sixty-two percent of his cancer patients told stories of loss, intense grief, depression, and despair that led up to their physical condition. As long ago as 1925, an analyst declared that after studying hundreds of cancer patients, she found most of them had suffered some important emotional crisis prior to the development of the disease, and that they had been unable to find effective outlets for their deep feelings and emotions.

LOVE HEALS AN EMPLOYER'S UNPLEASANTNESS

In the field of prosperity, love as impersonal good will is all-powerful, too. It has been estimated that only fifteen percent of a person's financial success is due to his technical ability, while eighty-five percent is due to his ability to get along with people. Personnel managers agree that more than two-thirds of the people who lose their jobs do so not because of incompetence, but because they cannot get along with others. Approximately ten percent are discharged because of inadequate preparation for the skills needed, whereas the other ninety percent are fired because of "personality problems."

A secretary once realized that in order to keep her job, which was interesting and well-paying, she would have to learn how to cope with her employer's unpleasant "morning disposition." She learned of the success power of

love and began using one of Emmet Fox's state-
ments: "ALL MEN ARE EXPRESSIONS OF DIVINE
LOVE; THEREFORE, I CAN MEET WITH NOTHING
BUT THE EXPRESSIONS OF DIVINE LOVE."[1]

Beginning her day with this statement helped
to establish a peaceful atmosphere in the office
for her employer's arrival. By the time he called
her in for dictation, divine love had done its
perfect work on his disposition. In time, his
morning grouchiness and moodiness were re-
placed with a consistent pleasant disposition.
The secretary felt her work in this regard was
highly worthwhile, since her boss' disposition
had been the only unfavorable and worrisome
aspect of her job.

LOVE PROSPERS A SALESMAN

Financially, an attitude of love is worthwhile,
too. A traveling salesman who was heavily in
debt attempted to get a loan from a bank to
pay off his debts. Because he lacked collateral,
he was not able to get the loan. He began to
affirm, "DIVINE LOVE PROSPERS ME NOW." Within a few days he made a large sale and was able
to pay off all his debts, with money left over.

---

1. From "Treatment for Divine Love" (card) by Emmet
Fox, published by DeVorss & Co., P.O. Box 550, Marina
del Rey, CA 90294.

HOW LOVE BROUGHT PROSPERITY IN
THE MIDST OF A RECESSION

A number of years ago during a financial recession, and in bitter cold weather, the firm for which I was working experienced financial difficulties. Members of the board of directors had become depressed because of the weather, which seemed to be delaying the firm's prosperity. They were also depressed about general economic conditions. It seemed a hopeless situation until several persons working for the firm agreed to begin affirming together, at specific times, statements on the prospering power of love. Each individual affirmed for himself and his own inspiration: "I AM THE LOVE OF GOD IN EXPRESSION, I LET GOD'S LOVE GUIDE, DIRECT, AND INSPIRE ME." The statement used for the firm's prosperity was: "GOD'S LOVE IN US IS DRAWING TO US NEW IDEAS, NEW COURAGE, AND VISIBLE DAILY SUPPLY. GOD'S LOVE IN YOU IS DRAWING TO YOU NEW IDEAS, NEW COURAGE, AND VISIBLE DAILY SUPPLY."

The atmosphere of depression and hopelessness concerning the business situation seemed to lift. Continued use of the prayers caused all those involved to experience an uplifted state of mind. New ideas and new courage attracted visible daily supply. Within a few weeks the financial crisis had passed, and that year proved to be one of the most prosperous the firm has ever known!

A chiropractor who was having similar financial challenges asked how this firm managed to make a financial comeback in the midst of bad weather and economic recession. The prayers were shared with him, and his financial results were so satisfying that he obtained a thousand printed copies of the prayers, which he distributed to his patients whenever they mentioned their own financial challenges. Thus the power of love proved its prospering power to many people that winter in our area alone.

HOW TO SUCCEED THROUGH LOVE

Many years ago, Emma Curtis Hopkins gave some financial advice along this line when she wrote, "Take your business as it is, and praise divine love that there is a strong, wise way out of your dilemma." When there is such a need, affirm, "I PRAISE DIVINE LOVE THAT THERE IS A STRONG, WISE WAY OUT OF THIS DILEMMA."

In all phases of life, love is a success power. Many people who are seeking a balanced life have found this prayer helpful: "DIVINE LOVE, EXPRESSING THROUGH ME, NOW DRAWS TO ME ALL THAT IS NEEDED TO MAKE ME HAPPY AND MY LIFE COMPLETE."

Whatever your need in life may be, love is the answer. You do not have to look outside yourself for love. Begin releasing it from within your own thoughts and feelings, and you will attract to you whatever people, situations, and conditions are for your highest good. Truly, "YOU WALK IN THE CHARMED CIRCLE OF GOD'S LOVE, AND YOU ARE DIVINELY IRRESISTIBLE TO YOUR HIGHEST GOOD NOW." This is the prospering power of love.

LOVE YOUR WAY TO SUCCESS

— Chapter 2 —

How often we try to battle our way through life, experiencing disappointment, pain, and failure at every turn, when we could much more easily love our way through life, experiencing success every step of the way!

Emmet Fox once wrote, "There is no difficulty that enough love will not conquer."[1]

I recall once having a problem that (I thought) I had tried in every way to solve. Still it was as though I faced a stone wall.

Other persons were involved. Until they took action, I was helpless to do anything more, I

1. From *Love* (card) by Emmet Fox, published by DeVorss & Co., Marina del Rey, CA 90294

reasoned. It seemed a particularly frustrating situation since the next move had to be made by someone else. I had prodded these persons in every way I knew and still they had not taken action. It seemed hopeless, until one day I read these words by Emma Curtis Hopkins:

> Everything is really full of love for you . . . The good that is for you loves you as much as you love it. The good that is for you seeks you and will come flying to you if you see that what you love is love itself. All people will change when you know that they are love. We shall change toward all people when we know that we ourselves are formed out of love. All is love. There is nothing in all the universe but love.

When I read those words, it was as though something hard broke up inside of me. I actually felt something hard move in the area of the heart; then it seemed to dissolve and I was able to breathe more freely.

Truly, there had been a stone wall in this situation, just as I had sensed. But that stone wall had not been an outer physical structure towering over me. The stone wall was actually within me, in the form of my own hard thoughts about the situation. It was a revelation, a surprise, and finally a relief to realize that not someone else, but my own hard thinking had been the barrier that had caused the situation to remain at a standstill.

I began to affirm: "EVERYTHING IS REALLY
FULL OF LOVE FOR ME, INCLUDING THOSE PERSONS.
THE GOOD THAT IS FOR ME IN THIS SITUATION
LOVES ME, AS MUCH AS I LOVE IT. THE GOOD
THAT IS FOR ME IN THIS MATTER NOW SEEKS ME,
AND COMES FLYING TO ME AS I BEHOLD THIS SITU-
ATION WITH LOVE."

Within a few days I heard from the persons
involved, though I had not heard from them
previously for many months. Their letter
seemed especially cordial, and it stated that
they were immediately expediting the matter in
which I was interested. Now, whenever I have
any business contact with this firm, they always
respond graciously and speedily. Never since
that time has there been any delay or misunderstanding.

You can love your way through any trouble-
some situation by declaring: "THIS PERSON AND
THIS SITUATION ARE REALLY FULL OF LOVE FOR
ME, AND I AM FULL OF LOVE FOR THEM. I PRAISE
DIVINE LOVE IN THIS MATTER NOW. I BEHOLD THIS
SITUATION WITH LOVE."

THE AUTHOR'S USE OF
LOVE AS A SECRET WEAPON
FOR SUCCESS

Some years ago I had another experience
that proved to me that there is nothing weak

about love; that love can win more battles than fists or weapons; that love is our "secret weapon" for successful results.

I was asked to take a job as director of a nonprofit organization. It was a job that no one else wanted because there had been great disharmony in this organization. Along with the ill feeling that had been generated, financial lack had also appeared. It was not a job to look forward to, especially since this would be my first assignment after entering a new field of work. I had proper training for the job, but no experience. This hardly seemed a suitable assignment for an inexperienced person, but it was this job or none for the present, so I reluctantly took it.

At the first meeting with the board of directors of the organization, things did not look promising. Two of the directors objected to my job appointment, saying that I was too young and inexperienced to straighten things out. Silently, I agreed with them wholeheartedly. But the other board members pointed out that I was the new director, having been trained and assigned to this job by the home office, and that they planned to work with me to straighten out difficulties in whatever way I felt best.

In praying for guidance about this challenging job, the thought came to me that divine love was to be my secret weapon; that love could win in this situation and could again

bring victorious results of harmony and prosperity to this organization.

When I expressed these thoughts at that first
board meeting, my ideas on divine love only
provoked the two objecting board members,
who scoffed at the "mere" power of love for
solving anything. They "told me off" for even
suggesting such a thing, and then they resigned. This proved to be love's first step in
clearing away inharmony.

In private conversation, the chairman of the
board of directors agreed with me that there
was nothing weak about divine love; that divine
love could win this battle. He believed so
strongly in the harmonizing, prospering power
of love to make things right that he agreed to
meet with me for an hour every morning so that
we might discuss the various affairs of the organization and affirm the perfect results of
divine love.

The affirmations we used in those daily
morning meetings were: "DIVINE LOVE IS DOING
ITS PERFECT WORK HERE AND NOW. DIVINE LOVE
HARMONIZES, DIVINE LOVE ADJUSTS, DIVINE LOVE
PROSPERS. DIVINE LOVE FORESEES EVERYTHING AND
RICHLY PROVIDES EVERY GOOD THING FOR THIS
ORGANIZATION NOW. DIVINE LOVE IS NOW
VICTORIOUS!"

The results of those daily meetings were
almost unbelievable. As we poured forth words
of divine love into this troubled situation, it was

like pouring out a healing balm. Attitudes and actions became quiet, peaceful, harmonious, cooperative. Soon it seemed as though there had never been any difficulty in the organization. Peace and harmony reigned in all its activities.

As we continued daily affirmations of divine love, new people, new activity, new prosperity flowed into this organization. The financial income soon doubled. A number of gifts came, including fresh paint and willing painters who applied it free of charge to the building. New drapes, lovely new furnishings, air conditioners, a public-address system, and other needed equipment were provided. The entire building that housed the organization was beautifully redecorated within a few months.

The organization went on to new growth, new progress, new prosperity. Soon no one spoke of or cared about the former trouble; everything was so wonderful in the present. Though I am no longer connected with that organization, it has continued to grow and prosper over the years. Divine love met and solved my challenges there; divine love has continued to do its perfect work in that group.

THE PROBLEM-SOLVING POWER OF LOVE

A housewife decided to use love as her secret weapon in a troublesome situation. For months she had been speaking of her "no-good" husband. He was a miner who left home every spring to find work in the gold and silver mines of the Northwest. Usually after he left for the mines, she did not hear from him again until late fall, when he came home to loaf all winter.

During the summer months, she was left at home alone to work as a waitress, or to do anything else she could to feed and clothe herself and pay the bills. She had been contemplating divorce because life with her husband seemed a hopelesss struggle for existence.

It was then that she learned of the problem-solving power of love. Instead of continuing to dwell upon her husband's faults, she began to decree that divine love was doing its perfect work in her marriage, in their financial affairs, and in her husband's job prospects. Good things began to happen.

Her husband wrote her that he had obtained work in a silver mine and that he would begin sending money home regularly when he received his first pay check. Since he had never previously sent money home, this seemed a miracle. Though in the past he had not written at all when he was away, he now wrote long, friendly letters regularly, even speaking of his desire for them to have a good life together.

At the end of the summer mining season he wrote that he had work for the winter, too. This was unusual since his type of work had always been seasonal. As his wife continued to affirm the perfect outworking of divine love, their marriage became completely harmonized, their debts of long standing were paid. Her husband formed his own mining corporation and went into business for himself. He helped her start her own business which she manages while he is away in the mines. It is a business that they work in together when he is not otherwise occupied.

How often people have missed the blessings and security of a happy marriage and a good life because they have condemned and criticized, rather than loved their way through the challenges that confronted them! Yet how much easier it is to love your way through a problem than to battle your way through it!

CRITICISM CAN BRING NEGATIVE RESULTS

The unloving, unnecessary results that people often bring on themselves through criticism (the opposite of love) recall the story of the young artist who had a genius (he thought) for picking out the faults and weaknesses of other people. He prided himself on seeing the unworthy traits in their character. One night this young man had a dream in which he saw himself walking on a barren road, struggling wearily beneath a heavy burden.

In the dream he cried out weakly: "What is this heavy weight I have to carry? Why must I carry it? Why should I be so burdened?" A voice answered: "Your burden is the weight of all the faults you have found in other people. Why do you complain? You discovered those faults. Should they not, therefore, belong to you?"

The description of evil doubles the appearance of evil. *Whatever of evil you see in others, you are inviting into your own life in some form of negation*. When you "run down" someone else with your criticism and condemnation, you are opening the way for your own mind, body, or affairs to become "run down" with ill health, unhappiness, confusion, or financial lack.

A group of employees withdrew from a business firm because they did not like the new manager. Then they continued to belittle and condemn the new manager after they were no longer connected with the firm. As they continued in their negative judgments, one of these former employees had a heart attack and died within a few months. Another former employee opened a new business; it soon failed. Later he opened several other businesses, and they failed. He also became estranged from several members of his family.

Other former employees of the firm who remained critical had similar destructive experiences to meet. One businesswoman had a stroke, developed paralysis, and passed on within a year, though she previously had enjoyed many healthy years of active living. Another person developed arthritis, and soon could walk only on crutches. Still another person had several bouts of pneumonia and had to be hospitalized frequently. Physical suffering was also attended by heavy financial expense, and by other business problems. *The unjust criticisms these people had meant for someone else hurt only themselves.*

As for the new manager, he was aware of the backstairs gossip but he ignored it, for he knew it had no power; and both he and his business prospered.

HOW TO HANDLE YOUR
INITIATIONS IN LOVE

The ancients knew another success secret we should know: The description of good doubles good! May Rowland in her book *Dare to Believe!* has described how you can double the good in your life:

> If you are not attracting the good that you desire in your life, learn to express love; become a radiating center of love; and you will find that love, the divine magnet within you,

will change your whole world. . . . When your heart is filled with love you will not be critical or irritable, but you will be divinely irresistible.[2]

Florence Scovel Shinn wrote, "Every man on this planet is taking his initiation in love."[3] *Whatever your problem, it is but a test in love. If you meet that test through love, your problem will be solved. If you do not meet that test through love, your problem will continue until you do! Your problem is your initiation in love.*

A businesswoman recently related how she met her initiation in love:

> Only a short time ago, I felt I could not go on. My husband was on the brink of a nervous breakdown and in deep depression. Our oldest son, age nineteen, was struggling to stay in college, doing it all on his own, without a dime of help from us. Our middle son, age twelve, had been under treatment for several years as an emotionally disturbed child. He has periods of becoming quite angry, on the edge of violence. Our daughter, age eleven, was beginning to react to all this discord with temper tantrums and sulking spells, and seemed unable to get along harmoniously with her friends or teach-

2. May Rowland, *Dare to Believe* (Unity Village, MO: Unity Books, 1961).
3. Florence Scovel Shinn, *The Game of Life and How to Play It* (Marina del Rey, CA: DeVorss & Co., 1925) p.26.

ers. I kept getting one kidney infection after another. Since I have only one kidney, you can understand the concern I felt when my doctor warned me to be especially careful.

After reading an article about the power of divine love to improve personalities, situations, events, even one's health, I bought a notebook and a pen. Every time I started to worry, feel sick or afraid, I sat down, relaxed, wrote the name of the family member or the situation that was bothering me, and then I wrote down a decree of love about it. For my husband, our children, and for myself, I often wrote over and over: "I BEHOLD YOU WITH THE EYES OF LOVE AND I GLORY IN YOUR PERFECTION."

The results were almost unbelievable! My husband was at a standstill when I began using the power of love on our affairs six weeks ago. Recently he took a bath, the first in weeks; he got his hair cut and turned out some work on his own, without a word of prodding from me. Our son in college received a one-hundred-dollar refund on income tax. He also got a job managing the baseball team, so his tuition will be provided. Our middle son has gone for several weeks now without displaying violent behavior. His disposition has greatly improved. Our daughter is getting along better with her friends and teachers. As for my kidney infection, it has cleared up completely, and I am now launching on a health program to build up my resistance. I have also obtained a part-time job. You can see why I shall always be grateful that I learned about the problem-solving power of love!

CALL FORTH LOVE TO OVERCOME
ALL DIFFICULTIES

Charles Fillmore has written:

The more we talk about love, the stronger it grows in the consciousness, and if we persist in thinking loving thoughts and speaking loving words, we are sure to bring into our experience the feeling of that great love that is beyond description — the very love of God. . . .

You may trust love to get you out of your difficulties. There is nothing too hard for it to accomplish for you, if you put your confidence in it.[4]

Love works in varied ways to produce right results, when it is recognized and called forth in a situation. As you begin to think more about how you can love your way through life, rather than about how you have to battle your way through life, love will reveal to you its secret success powers. Launch forth on the great venture of love, and affirm often along the way: "I LIVE BY THE LAW OF LOVE, AND LOVE IS NOW VICTORIOUS." This one thought can win many a battle in your life.

---

4. Charles Fillmore, *Talks on Truth* (Unity Village, MO: Unity books, 1926) p.51.

LOVE WORKS A HEALING POWER

— Chapter 3 —

Part of the spring season is the religious observance of Lent, usually considered a period of prayer and fasting, which symbolizes a time of preparation for the resurrection of new life and beauty in one's personal world.

Let us stop crucifying and start resurrecting during the Lenten season and all through the the year! We can do it through the healing power of love.

What you should do is fast from negative memories of the past—grudges, criticisms, spite, feelings of injustice and hurt, as well as other inharmonies. There are definite, simple ways you can pour out the healing power of love on your negative memories, so that you can be free of them forever. As you do become free of these destructive emotions, you cease crucifying yourself and others and you are then ready for resurrected good.

A businesswoman in France reported:

My aunt is responding at last to the waves of divine love I have been radiating to her. She now refers to me as her "beloved niece." This was a very negative relationship that divine love has now reversed!

SPECIAL PHASES OF LOVE: FORGIVENESS AND RELEASE

There are two special ways you can fast from negative attitudes, and tune in on the healing power of love, which makes you whole in mind, body, and affairs. These special ways are the act of release, and the act of forgiveness. Perhaps it surprises you to hear that release and forgiveness are parts of love. Yet *when you find that other phases of love have not healed some troublesome condition in your life, you may discover that it is because you have not invoked the releasing, forgiving phases of love.* When you do, satisfying results will surely come.

Kahlil Gibran might have been describing these two important phases of love when he wrote: "Speak to us of love. . . . Even as he [love] is for your growth so is he for your pruning . . . think not you can direct the course of love, for love, if it finds you worthy, directs your course."[1]

You have heard it said that love is a many-splendored thing, but often when the pruning power of love is at work in your life you may have felt that love is a "many-splintered" thing. When you are willing to release and forgive, the splinter (or "thorn in the flesh") is transformed into a splendid result, and you find that love is able to direct your course to greater good.

Through release and forgiveness you break up, cross out, dissolve, and are freed forever from the negative attitudes and memories that have limited you to less than the highest and best in your life experience.

The freeing, forgiving attitude likewise "raises" your good and brings it to life. Invoke the healing power of love through freeing and forgiving the negative experiences of your past and present, and you will find yourself well on the way to resurrected good.

---

1. Reprinted from *The Prophet*, by Kahlil Gibran, with permission of the publisher, Alfred A. Knopf, Inc., Copyright 1923 by Kahlil Gibran; renewal copyright 1951 by Administrators C.T.A. of Kahlil Gibran estate, and Mary G. Gibran.

It is the spiritual law that you must forgive if you want to demonstrate over your own difficulties and make any real progress in life. Many people consider *forgive* an unpleasant word, but it means simply to set free, to liberate, by "giving" something positive in place of or "for" something negative.

RELEASE IS A FORM OF FORGIVENESS

Release is a form of forgiveness that we all need to practice often. Although we usually think of emotional attachment as one of the highest forms of love, quite the opposite is true. Emotional *release* is one of the highest forms of love. Attachment leads to bondage, whereas the way of true love is to free that which you love. *You never lose anything through release. Instead, you open the way for a freer, more satisfying type of love to develop, where everyone involved is able to give and receive love in a more harmonious way.*

You never lose that which is for your highest good, under any circumstances. When it seems that you have lost something, it is because it is no longer best for you. Though you may feel that it is still best, you have actually outgrown it, and the pruning power of love has released you from it. Realizing this, you are able to free it and open your mind and heart to receive your new and higher good.

Setting others free means setting yourself free. When you feel bound to other people, their attitudes, their behavior, their way of life, it is because you are (perhaps unconsciously) binding them to you. Then you begin to feel bound, chafing against the very bondage you have caused! Always you yourself hold the key to your freedom from bondage. You turn the key to that freedom when you release the personality, problem, or condition that you think is clutching you. Remember you are the master, never the slave, of circumstances.

You become victor instead of victim when you dare to speak the word of release to the person or thing you think is binding you. You are your own bondage made manifest. You can become your own release made manifest, too.

A businesswoman in Florida wrote:

> I was especially interested to read in *The Prospering Power of Love* that when you are in a situation where you are being dominated, it is because *you* have formed a "binding action" and you need to "forgive and release."
>
> After I read this, and daily practiced release, an inharmonious work situation became friendly and comfortable. Releasing, forgiving, and loving: these prayer methods have blessed me beyond all my expectations!

THE HEALING POWER OF RELEASE

A housewife had worried for many months over her husband's illness. The more she tried to help him recover, the more he seemed to cling to his illness and the more confined they both were. One day she learned of the healing power of release and began to declare for her husband: "I RELEASE YOU NOW TO YOUR HIGHEST GOOD. I LOVE YOU BUT I RELEASE YOU TO COMPLETE FREEDOM AND COMPLETE HEALTH IN WHATEVER WAY IS BEST. I AM FREE AND YOU ARE FREE."

When this woman had previously tried to help her husband by using various healing affirmations, he had seemed subconsciously to resist her attempts to will him to health. After she began to release him to find health in his own way, ceasing any mental effort in his direction, and began to lead a more normal life herself, her husband's health rapidly improved. Some of his former ailments disappeared completely. He experienced the healing power of love as it worked through release.

Most human-relations problems would melt away if people would practice the healing power of release, instead of trying to make people over in a certain image, or trying to force them to do things in a certain way.

Nowhere is there more need for the expression of love as release than between husbands

and wives, between parents and children. We
often try to bend others to our will, calling it
love when it is really selfish possessiveness that
binds instead of frees. Then we wonder why
others resist instead of accepting our "help."

Gibran described the loving attitude of release in marriage: "Love one another, but make
not a bond of love . . . let there be spaces in
your togetherness. . . . Sing and dance together
and be joyous, but let each one of you be alone
. . . stand together yet not too near together."[2]

He described the loving attitude of release toward children in these words: "Your children
are not your children. They are the sons and
daughters of Life's longing for itself. They
come through you but not from you, and
though they are with you yet they belong not to
you. . . . You may house their bodies but not
their souls. . . . You may strive to be like them,
but seek not to make them like you."[3]

A MOTHER-DAUGHTER RELATIONSHIP
HEALED THROUGH RELEASE

A counselor was once called to a hospital to
visit a young woman who had experienced a ner-

2. Gibran, *The Prophet*.
3. Ibid.

vous breakdown. She was having severe headaches and prolonged crying spells. Drugs and
medication had brought no relief.

Her mother was frantic with fear, saying: "I
can't understand what has happened. This girl
has always been such an obedient child. She has
never disagreed with me, nor crossed me in any
way. But now she is saying terrible things to me.
She tells me I've ruined her life, that I have
kept her from getting a job and working; that
I've kept her from marrying and having a normal life. To be sure, I never encouraged her to
work, because she had always been a timid,
sickly child. There was no financial reason for
her to work, and so I insisted that she remain at
home and help out there, thinking it would
provide her with a more pleasant way of life.
Now she is criticizing and condemning me for
it. She suddenly seems to hate me."

Her daughter, who was finally rebelling
against her mother's domination and "smother
love," was hardly a child. She was past thirty,
though she still wore bobby socks, long hair,
and teen-age clothes. She also seemed to think
and talk like a teenager.

The daugher felt quite guilty about having
turned against her mother, but she said she
could not help it. When assured by the counselor that she was reacting in a normal way, she
began to relax. As she did, the severe headaches

left her completely. Her crying ceased. She was
able to retain food again, and her strength returned. Much of the hostility toward her mother
soon faded away.

Further talks with this mother and daughter
helped them both to realize that this experience
had been for the good. Had this daughter not
been able to release her accumulated hostilities
toward her mother, had she not been able to
begin claiming her emotional independence,
she would doubtless have faced confinement in
a mental hospital. The statistics of mental illness show that most of it arises from inharmonious relationships in the home — relationships
that are usually possessive and dominating.
Mental illness is the patient's way of fighting
that domination and escaping from
possessiveness.

Your dear ones must have liberty to live their
own lives, and you must grant it to them, or
else you will create problems for them and for
yourself. *If you want to free yourself from all
types of problems in mind, body, and affairs,
you must release others to find their good in
their own way.* A clear channel is then opened
for a great good to come to all involved. Your
own freedom and well-being depend upon such
release, as do the freedom and well-being of
your loved ones.

RELEASE FREES A MOTHER AND SON

A professional woman was quite concerned about her bachelor son. He was very successful in his work but had never married, and still lived with his mother. A widow, she devoted many years of her life to rearing and educating this son. Now the time had come when she wished to be free to travel and perhaps to work elsewhere. She also longed to see her son happily married. She realized that her own freedom and well-being depended upon such emotional release of her son.

Then it seemed that her dreams were coming true: her son met the girl of his choice. But instead of being happy about it, his mother became upset and resentful, constantly finding fault with the girl. Soon she became ill, and her physician told her that she was suffering from hypertension caused by some secret anxiety.

She then realized that in order to be free from illness, in order to live a happy, balanced life, she must free her son to live his life as he wished. She realized that setting him free meant setting herself free. For this purpose she constantly affirmed: "I FULLY AND FREELY RELEASE YOU. I LOOSE YOU AND LET YOU GO TO YOUR GOOD. THE GOOD OF ONE IS THE GOOD OF ALL." Before long all anxiety left her, her health improved, and her son was married. This left her free to

travel, to seek new work, and to develop a whole
new, freer way of life that she had long wanted.

*When your prayers have not been answered,
it is often because you need to practice release—
release of some person or situation, some financial or health problem.* Often it is not an enemy
you need to release but a friend, a relative—a
husband, wife, or child. As you practice
release, your problem is solved, your good is
resurrected.

YOU MUST FORGIVE FOR
YOUR OWN SAKE

Forgiveness is a very important type of release, and a most important form of love. When
you practice forgiveness, you experience the
healing power of love. You must forgive injuries
and hurts of the past and present—not so much
for the other person's sake as for your own. Resentment, condemnation, anger, the desire to
"get even" or to see someone punished or hurt,
are things that rot your soul. They bind you to
many other problems which actually have
nothing to do with the original grievances.

Emmet Fox has explained: "When you hold
resentment against anyone, you are bound to
that person by a cosmic link, a real though mental chain. You are tied by a cosmic tie to the

thing that you hate. The one person perhaps in the whole world whom you most dislike is the very one to whom you are attaching yourself by a hook that is stronger than steel."[4]

A HOUSEWIFE'S FORGIVENESS BRINGS HEALING AND PROSPERITY

A housewife recently described how the healing power of love worked in her family through forgiveness: "Ten months ago my whole world seemed to have crashed to pieces. My husband's job, managerial in nature, was suddenly (and apparently unfairly) terminated. Two of our children and I were very sick with bronchial infections. I also had a recurrence of a bladder infection. It was at this hopeless point in our affairs that I was introduced to one of the Ponder prosperity books, which I began to study. In it I read something I needed very much: 'I FULLY AND FREELY FORGIVE. I LOOSE AND LET GO. I CAST ALL JUDGMENTS, RESENTMENTS, CRITICISM, AND UNFORGIVENESS UPON THE CHRIST WITHIN, TO BE DISSOLVED AND HEALED. THE PROSPERING TRUTH

---

4. *The Sermon on the Mount* (New York: Harper & Row, 1938) p.188.

HAS SET ME FREE TO MEET MY RICH GOOD AND TO
SHARE MY GOOD WITH OTHERS!'

"As I read these words, I realized I had been
openly resentful toward my husband's former
employer because of his seeming unfairness and
poor business judgement. I kept using the affirmations in the book and actually it became
very easy to forgive completely.

"Within the next few days my infection was
gone, a skin ailment of my mother's disappeared, and then our financial demonstrations
began! Our debts had seemed insurmountable;
but gradually, through a complete change of
mind brought about by forgiveness, money began to come from unexpected sources. We received an income tax refund; my parents sent
money to cover the rent; our creditors did not
press us for money. After being unemployed for
two months, my husband was led to the right
job, one which he thoroughly understands, as
general manager of a ski resort which is under
construction now and which we will move to
shortly. The corporation is building us a wonderful apartment, fully carpeted and decorated
to our taste."

*When we hold resentment toward another,
we are bound to that person or condition by a
cosmic link, and forgiveness is the only way to
dissolve that link and be free.*

WHAT IT MEANS WHEN OTHERS
HURT OR DISAPPOINT YOU

Since other persons are children of God, there is really nothing to forgive. They have not really failed us, or disappointed us, or let us down, or shamed us. They may have stumbled while crossing our pathway. But they were sons of God who had temporarily lost their way. If they crossed our pathway, it was because they needed and wanted our blessing. They were unconsciously looking to us to be steadied and set right.

Our progress has not been hindered, no matter what they did or did not do. They did not, they could not, keep our good from us. They crossed our path by divine appointment, even though they seemed to hurt us for a little while. *When people bother us in any way, it is because their souls are trying to get our divine attention, and our blessing. When we give them that, they no longer bother us. They fade out of our lives and find their good elsewhere.*

A nurse found great comfort and truth in these words, after she was seriously injured in a collision with a car driven by an intoxicated man. After recovering she returned to her nursing profession. Again and again the man responsible for the collision was admitted to the hospital where she worked — and always he was in an intoxicated state. She refused to nurse him, and was assured by his doctor that she would not be assigned to his case.

Once when he was admitted, there was a shortage of nurses on her floor, and she was the only nurse available when the light came on in his room. Since it was unavoidable, she took him his tray and medicine. When she appeared, he recognized her, talked about the accident, and told her he had been worried about her financial affairs after the accident, realizing that she was widowed with children to care for.

In the wee hours of the morning, as they talked, he asked her forgiveness, and she gave it. The amazing thing was that, following their conversation, he gradually stopped drinking, and she never heard of his being admitted to the hospital again. She realized that the man seemed to have wanted her forgiveness and blessing . When he got that, he faded out of her life.

HOW A LUMP WAS HEALED

If you do not know what or who it is you need to forgive, when your good seems withheld from you ask God to reveal to you what or whom you need to forgive. You may be surprised to find where the block is!

A woman discovered a lump in her breast and was greatly frightened by it. But instead of rushing out to talk about it to anyone, she decided to analyze the situation mentally and pray for guidance.

She realized that a hard condition in the body symbolizes a hard condition in the mind— hard thoughts of resentment, condemnation, unforgiveness. She prayed, "Divine Intelligence, what or whom do I need to forgive?

Since the answer did not come immediately, she continued every day to pray, meditate, and ask: "Divine Intelligence, what or whom do I need to forgive? What hard attitudes do I need to release, give up, in order to be forgiven this condition?" In meditation one day she found herself thinking about her husband and a woman with whom he had been involved five years previously. At the time, she had met the experience nonresistantly, and it had faded away. She and her husband were now happier than ever, but she realized in this meditation period that she still had hard thoughts toward the other woman and toward her husband concerning the distressing experiences during that period.

She prayed for the other woman, blessed her, released her, saying to her mentally: "I FREELY

FORGIVE YOU, I LET YOU GO. YOU HAVE GONE TO
MEET YOUR GOOD AND TO SHARE YOUR GOOD ELSE-
WHERE. IT IS DONE, IT IS FINISHED." To her hus-
band she mentally said: "I FREELY FORGIVE YOU.
I LET GO ALL FALSE CONCEPTS ABOUT YOU. YOU
ARE A FAITHFUL, LOVING HUSBAND, AND WE HAVE
A WONDERFUL MARRIAGE. ONLY GOOD HAS COME
FROM THAT EXPERIENCE."

She declared these words of forgiveness in her
prayer time for several weeks. One day she realized that the lump in her breast was gone; she
never knew when it disappeared.

A SURE REMEDY FOR RESURRECTING
HEALTH, WEALTH AND HAPPINESS

Deliberately practice the healing power of
love through acts of forgiveness and release.
Charles Fillmore describes this as a "sure remedy" for resurrecting health, wealth, and happiness:

Bless your problem, whatever it be, with a
thought somewhat like this: "I NOW RELEASE
YOU AND BLESS YOU. DIVINE LOVE IS ADJUSTING MY
LIFE AND ITS PROBLEMS. REALIZING THIS, I ABIDE
IN PEACE.". . . Every person who thus allies
himself with the power of divine love creates a
bit of heaven on earth.[5]

5. From the pamphlet, *A Sure Remedy*, by Charles Fillmore, published by Unity School of Christianity, Unity
Village, MO 64065.

A schoolteacher in Oklahoma confirmed this when she wrote:

I have given my niece a copy of *The Prospering Power of Love,* and she recently spent an entire afternoon telling me how that book has revolutionized her life.

She and her husband of forty years had been having some serious marital difficulties. So she decided to work for a whole month on forgiveness, as outlined in the book.

When her husband returned home from his traveling job, at the end of that month, his entire attitude had changed. He told her how lovely she looked. He asked how she had managed to lose ten pounds, and he said she appeared more relaxed. His pleasant attitudes seemed a miracle.

THE RESURRECTING POWER OF LOVE

— Chapter 4 —

The word *resurrect* means "to bring to view again . . . to restore to life." The resurrection of Jesus Christ was for the purpose of bringing to view again the divine nature of all mankind.

Man was created with a divine nature, in the image of God. But man misused his divine nature by turning his attention to a belief in evil, and so man forgot about his divinity or how to use it.

Some of the great characters of the Old Testament tried to bring back to notice, to use, the divine nature of man. David sang of man's divinity: "Yet thou hast made him little less than God, and dost crown him with glory and

57

honor" (Psalms 8:5). "You are gods, Sons of the Most High, all of you" (Psalms 82:6). Job realized, "There is a spirit in man" (Job 32:8).

Spiritual man has always been crowned with glory and honor, though mankind lost sight of its glorious divinity for many centuries. In order to bring to view again, to restore to life, man's divinity, a loving Father sent a Savior, a Redeemer — one who would resurrect the divinity of all mankind.

YOU CAN BE FREED FROM ALL KINDS OF LIMITATION

The raising up of the Christ nature in the man Jesus symbolizes the resurrection of the Christ nature in all mankind. Jesus described man's divinity when He said, "The kingdom of God is in the midst of you" (Luke 17:21). *What theology calls a "lost soul" is merely a soul that has lost sight of its divinity. When our divine nature is brought back into view, into use, it can lift us out of all kinds of limitation.*

A housewife from Pennsylvania wrote:

> I had a copy of *The Prospering Power of Love* in my pocketbook when I visited my daughter in the hospital. I noticed how depressed a young lady was in the next bed, so I offered her my

book. She accepted it gladly, and here is the note she wrote me later:

> "I can't thank you enough for sharing with me *The Prospering Power of Love.* I am not a religious fanatic, but God has changed my life immensely since I began study of that book, and learned that I have a divine nature. If I had not been introduced to those ideas and used them, I would be in bad shape today, both mentally and physically. Instead I am well on the way to total recovery in every way."

A statement I have used many times over the years, one that has helped lift me out of limitation, is this: "CHRIST IN ME NOW FREES ME FROM ALL LIMITATION. I AM THE RESURRECTION AND THE LIFE."

Paul said that this resurrected Christ nature in man is the mystery that has been hidden for generations, and he described it as man's hope of glory. He reminded the early Christians of their divinity: "Do you not know that your body is a temple of the Holy Spirit within you, which you have from God? . . . So glorify God in your body" (1 Corinthians 6:19,20).

Charles Fillmore described resurrection as the "raising up of the whole man—spirit, soul, and body—into the Christ consciousnesss of life and wholeness." He wrote in *Keep a True Lent*:

> The time is ripe for the advent of a new race, the advent of the spiritualized man. This

will be brought about not by a miracle or the fiat of God, but by the gradual refinement of the man of the flesh into the man of Spirit. The true overcomer is qualifying himself to become a member of the new spiritualized race.[1]

Just as Jesus, through His resurrection of His spiritual nature, brought back into notice this spiritualized man, so we can bring alive the divinity within us, and in other people. As we do, we become a part of the spiritualized race which overcomes or "comes up over" the negative experiences of life.

"Think of yourself in a large way, and the little things of life will lose interest for you," says Charles Fillmore. "See all things from the large viewpoint. Instead of seeing yourself as mere man, see yourself as divine being. The only difference between gods and men is in comprehension. Men have the power to comprehend and appropriate all they have imagined possible with God."

HOW PRAISE CAN EXPAND YOUR GOOD

From a practical standpoint, you can see yourself and others in a large way, as divine

1. Published by Unity School of Christianity, Unity Village, MO 64065 (1953).

beings, through praise. Praise is one of the strongest forms of love. Praise expands your good. Praise is your resurrecting power because it brings back into notice and use, back to life, the good in yourself and in others. Ella Wheeler Wilcox was expressing the highest form of praise in her poem "Attainment" when she wrote,

> "Know that you are great,
> Great with divinity."

The word *praise* means to express approval, to glorify, to appraise as good. When you express approval of yourself or others, you are glorifying the divine in yourself and others. Always you can resurrect or bring back to notice the good, the divinity in people and situations through praise.

Say to yourself often: "THROUGH THE POWER OF CHRIST IN ME, MY LIFE CAN BE AS WONDERFUL AS I WANT IT TO BE!" Whether it seems to be literally true or not, begin to think of yourself as glorious, splendid, beloved, strong, well, capable. Begin to think of the world as a beautiful place in which to live, work, grow, play. Affirm often for others, especially those who trouble you: "THROUGH THE POWER OF CHRIST IN YOU, YOUR LIFE CAN BE AS WONDERFUL AS YOU WANT IT TO BE!" You will be surprised how this simple, delightful way of thinking will resurrect — bring back to notice, restore to life — your good. Also, declare often for any situation that troubles you: "I APPRAISE THIS SITUATION AS GOOD."

A BOOKKEEPER IMPROVED HER
EMPLOYER'S DISPOSITION

I once knew of an employer for whom no one liked to work. This solemn, serious man was irritable, impatient, hard to please. One bookkeeper who had worked for him for many years finally had to resign because of ill health. Everyone wondered what would become of the employer, since nobody wanted the bookkeeper's job. None of the local townspeople applied for it.

Instead, an out-of-town bookkeeper took the job. She was a happy, jolly, attractive person, quite in contrast to the serious, drab, complaining person who had previously worked for this man. She obviously expected to have a good time in her new job. She was appraising the situation as good.

She planned each day around her new employer's well-being. She came in early to beautify his office and set things in order before beginning the day. She often brought fresh flowers for his desk from her garden. She inquired about how he wanted everything done and made it a point to please him. She often complimented him on some aspect of his work, or perhaps on his wife and family. By making things as pleasant as possible, the bookkeeper slowly transformed her employer into a calm, peaceful, happy individual.

For the first time in years, he smiled regularly and genuinely. It was a joy to those about him to observe him so happy and relaxed. In his appreciation he loosened his purse strings and gave the new employee several raises. Soon she was making more money than his previous bookkeeper had made. This happy state of affairs continued for some time until the bookkeeper's husband was transferred to an out-of-state position, and she left her job to join him. On her last day in the office, her boss actually cried softly. He held a luncheon in her honor and gave her a substantial bonus check as a going away gift.

The next bookkeeper who came to work for this man knew nothing of appraising people and situations as good, thereby resurrecting the good in them. She knew nothing of the magic power of praise and approval. The result was that the employer retreated into his shell of unpleasantness and soon regained his title of many years' standing as the hardest man in town to work for.

When you see beauty, life, pleasantness springing up all around in the wonders of nature, use often the resurrecting power of love through praise. Express approval of others, appraise situations as good regardless of appearances, and glorify your own appearance and your world. As you do so, you will become a part of the resurrecting power of love that is mightily at work in every atom of the universe.

YOU CAN MULTIPLY BEAUTY IN
YOUR APPEARANCE AND WORLD

You can glorify your own appearance and that of your world by creating as much beauty as possible. A famous actress was once asked how she stayed so young, though she was actually past seventy. Her reply was that she remained youthful by looking at beauty, appreciating beauty, thinking about beauty.

You can have more beauty in your world if you will begin right where you are to add whatever touches of beauty are possible. As you do this, beauty will multiply in your life. As you dwell more and more on beauty and do all that is possible to produce it in your world, you will become more successful and prosperous.

Once I found myself in a situation where there seemed to be no beauty. One room looked especially hopeless. It was a clutter of old, worn-out, discarded furniture. A friend who knew of the resurrecting power of beauty kept looking at that cluttered room, too. We could not decide what possible use could be made of it, for it seemed so unsightly. Finally we decided to "form a vacuum" by getting rid of all the old furniture, drapes, and rugs.

Almost immediately after the room was emptied, ideas began to come for its redecoration. As the ideas came, we were able to find one item that fitted our redecoration theme. We bought that piece and placed it in the empty room. That one beautiful object was like a magnet. It quickly drew other beautiful objects, as gifts. Money came easily for more costly items to create an elegant atmosphere. Everything and everybody seemed to want to enhance the beauty of that room. Soon it was the most beautiful room in the entire building. People often visited that room just to feed on its beauty. They said that it gave them a sense of peace, serenity, well-being. Soon the essence of beauty in that room seemed to permeate the entire building, and redecoration of other rooms took place.

An interior decorator in California wrote:

> The book, *The Prospering Power of Love*, was loaned to me by a friend, and it helped me to solve a knotty business problem.

Now when I speak to groups on interior design, I always read the passage on how the author created a beautiful room. My audiences always love that story! It gives them such hope for beautifying and expanding their own worlds.

You can use this method for building a beautiful wardrobe of clothes, or for furnishing your home or office. Begin by getting one truly elegant item that delights you and makes you feel rich. If it is an item of clothing, wear it often, mentally appreciating it, and it will open the way for other lovely clothes to be yours.

By fixing your attention on one beautiful item, you create the mental image of beauty, and that image goes to work through you and through others to create more beauty for you. The important thing is to make a start toward beauty, even in a small way. As you do, beauty multiplies for you, and you are able to resurrect beauty and to glorify your life and your world.

THE HEALING POWER OF BEAUTY

Beauty also has resurrecting power for health. When you are trying to achieve freedom from aches and pains, that is the time to wear your brightest, light-colored clothes. The body seems to respond to bright, light colors that suggest life, health, vitality.

Color-healing is an ancient science that is now being rediscovered. It was practiced in the healing temples of ancient Egypt, India, and China. Experiments have recently been made in some of our modern hospitals to learn the effect of color on a patient's recovery. Particularly in mental hospitals is color therapy known to be effective.

A schoolteacher, following an automobile accident, broke out with a painful rash which medical treatment failed to alleviate. It was suggested that she begin giving thanks for the perfect healing in a joyous, happy manner, and that she wear her prettiest, brightest clothes every day until she was healed. It was suggested that instead of staying home and trying to hide the rash, she should get into a party mood and have a good time. It sounded like a ridiculous prescription for healing. But it worked.

A woman who had suffered for months with various aches and pains found that neither medical nor metaphysical treatment seemed to help, until it was suggested that she stop wearing the dark clothes she had worn for months. As she put on light, bright-colored clothes, her body seemed to rejoice in being clothed in beauty, and her aches and pains faded away. She also looked younger, and this helped her mentally to accept a perfect healing. An appropriate affirmation for this purpose is "I POUR

OUT UPON MY BODY TEMPLE THE OIL OF LOVE AND
CLOTHE IT IN GARMENTS OF PRAISE."

THERE'S HEALING POWER IN JOY

Another way to glorify your divinity and resurrect your good is through joy. Emma Curtis
Hopkins has described the resurrecting power
of joy. "Exaltation is a magnet for all good
things of the universe to hasten to you. Depression and anxiety are a magnet for trouble to fly
to you. . . . There is no power of healing in a
depressed state of mind. . . . In order to work
your best, metaphysically, you must be in an
exalted state of mind."

A woman who had experienced great sorrow
in her life gave in to despondency, insomnia,
and depression. Finally her physician informed
her that she would have to overcome her depression, which was affecting her health. He advised
her that the way to conquer depression was to
laugh at least three times a day, whether she
felt like it or not.

Though it seemed ridiculous to follow this
advice, she began retiring to her room three
time daily for the sole purpose of laughing and
making merry, whether there was actually
anything to laugh about or not. She was soon in
excellent health again, and her previously sor-
rowful life took on a happy new look.

Charles Fillmore has written: "All healing systems recognize joy as a beneficent factor in the restoration of health to the sick. . . . That there is an intimate relation between happiness and health goes without question."[2]

A business executive had a sudden attack of acute indigestion. He decided to see if joy would heal him. He had heard a lecturer say, "If you can manage to smile continuously for just five minutes, you can cure any pain." He went to the mirror and stood there smiling, timing himself by his watch to be sure he held the smile for five minutes. By the end of the five minutes, he was so amused at this method that he was laughing aloud. Suddenly he thought of the acute pain he had experienced just five minutes earlier. It was gone!

Fun, laughter, and joy are among the world's cheapest and best medicines. Give yourself large doses of these often. They will not only save you expensive medical bills, they will make your body healthier and your life happier.

JOYOUS ATTITUDES TOWARD OTHERS CAN HEAL THEM

If a person does not know of the resurrecting power of maintaining a joyous, pleasant frame

---

2. *Jesus Christ Heals* (Unity Village, MO 64065: Unity School of Christianity, 1939).

of mind, someone near him can still help resurrect his good by maintaining a joyous attitude about his life and affairs.

A popular radio announcer was warned that he would die of cancer. When the doctors told his wife that he had cancer and could not possibly live, she replied: "Tell me no more. I refuse to accept that diagnosis. My husband is too fine a man to die. He still has so much to give the world. I have faith that my husband is going to be healed." She continued to maintain this pleasant, faith-filled attitude.

Not only did the man have cancer; he was also an alcoholic. When relatives and friends had tried earlier to console his wife about his drinking, she had not accepted their sympathy. Instead she had replied: "My husband is too fine a man to be addicted to alcohol. He is going to be healed."

When her husband was sent home from the hospital, his case diagnosed as hopeless, he and his wife joined a prayer group that believed in spiritual healing. Many of his radio listeners were also praying for his healing. Through consistent prayer, he was healed of cancer and also of the desire to drink.

A famous television personality learned of the announcer's healing of cancer. Since the television star had recently had an operation for cancer and his future seemed uncertain, he wrote the announcer asking his secret for having made such a successful comeback. The announcer wrote back: "In the first place, don't believe any diagnosis you are given, unless you are told you can be healed. Refuse to believe anything else. Then pray daily, asking God what it is in life your are really supposed to do, and *joyously* get busy doing it!"

This series of events took place several years ago. Both the radio announcer and the television personality are still well and active in their careers.

YOUR LIFE CAN BECOME AS WONDERFUL AS YOU WANT IT TO BE

Lowell Fillmore once described the resurrecting power of joyous, happy words:

Good words taken into our mouth bring happiness and prosperity into our life, while . . . angry words interfere with the digestive processes in our stomach and upset other functions of our body. When you give someone a good tongue-lashing you harm yourself more than you do your target. . . . There is no nourishment in words of criticism concerning evil. . . . Neither can you grow and prosper on hard words. . . . Let your conversation be composed of words that are filled with the constructive vitamins of Spirit. . . . So when you have anything good to say, say it for goodness' sake.

Just as nature comes alive through the expression of beauty and joy, you can bring back to notice, to use, to life the divinity within you through the expression of beauty and joy. Express the resurrecting power of love often by affirming: "THROUGH THE POWER OF CHRIST WITHIN ME, MY LIFE CAN BE AS WONDERFUL AS I WANT IT TO BE! I POUR OUT UPON MY BODY TEMPLE THE OIL OF LOVE AND CLOTHE IT IN GARMENTS OF PRAISE. I APPRAISE OTHERS AS GOOD AS I AFFIRM FOR THEM: 'THROUGH THE POWER OF CHRIST IN YOU, YOUR LIFE CAN BE AS WONDERFUL AS YOU WANT IT TO BE.' I SAY IT FOR GOODNESS' SAKE. AND I GIVE THANKS THAT WE ARE ALL GREAT — GREAT WITH DIVINITY!"

A SPECIAL METHOD OF LOVE

Part I

— Chapter 5 —

It is one of the basic teachings of Truth that all environments, circumstances, and conditions that we experience existed first as ideas in our own mind, either consciously or subconsciously. One of the great secrets of love is to learn how to clear inharmonious ideas from our own consciousness, for this in turn clears inharmonious experiences and relationships from our life. *If you deal in the right way with your own thinking, the people around you will move into right conditions—either in your midst or by moving out of your life.* In one way or another, harmony will be established.

I want to share with you a special method for getting your thinking into divine order, promptly and surely. This mystical prayer method can add years to your life, as it relieves you of unnecessary worry and friction. It can work wonders in your relationships with others. It may even turn enemies into friends. And it will surely add immeasurably to your own mental and physical health, and wealth.

HOW THIS METHOD WORKS

You can employ this special method of love secretly — with words. True words are angels. True words are alive with good, and they produce good. But there is a definite method by which you can employ words and produce angelic results: by thinking of the person you are concerned about as having an angel or higher self (spiritual-self), to whom you write.

By writing to a person's angel, you establish in your own thinking a harmonious belief about that person: you radiate your harmonious feeling to that person subconsciously; and you also recognize and bring alive in that person's consciousness his own higher, spiritual self.

There is special power in writing to the angel of a person with whom you cannot reason or help in the usual ways. *There is something about written words of Truth that reaches to the judgment seat of such a person, getting past the emotional blocks of vanity, pride, deception, intellectual arguments, and penetrating his God-self.*

YOUNG DOCTOR PROVES THIS METHOD

I have known a number of persons who have used this special method of love for reaching troublesome people and clearing up inharmony. A young doctor recently learned of this method. For some months he had been out of harmony with another doctor and had used every means he knew to restore harmony, but the other physician had rebuffed his bids for reconciliation. The young doctor began writing daily to the angel of the other man, asking that perfect understanding be reestablished between them. Later the other doctor met him on the street, greeted him graciously, and invited him to lunch. Now they are again good friends.

RECONCILIATION ACHIEVED WITH STEPMOTHER

After their parents' divorce, two daughters went to live with their father and new stepmother. For a time it seemed a sticky situation with tension, resentment and hostility being expressed. These daughters tearfully reported this unhappy situation to their mother, who lived in another state. Her first reaction was one of helplessness and frustration. Then she remembered the miracle power of the angel-writing prayer method, and quietly suggested her daughters use it.

As they began to write daily to their own angels and to that of their stepmother, the tension and resentment melted away. Words of apology and notes of love were exchanged, followed by hugs and kisses. Happy tears were shed. Later their mother said, "It is a joy to feel the happiness my daughters are now experiencing with their father and stepmother."

A WONDER-WORKING TECHNIQUE

I have written about this mystical writing-to-the-angel method in an earlier edition of *The Prospering Power of Love*, as well as in my books, *The Dynamic Laws of Healing*, and *Pray and Grow Rich*. This secret prayer method can work wonders in your life — and in the lives of others!

I first learned of this secret prayer method from studying the mystical, yet practical writings of Emma Curtis Hopkins.[1] She was known as the "teacher of teachers" in the metaphysical field at the turn of the century, and taught this secret prayer method in her master classes in Chicago, San Francisco, and other cities around the country. Fifty thousand people studied with her at the turn of the century, long before radio, television and other mass-media methods of communication were available. The Fillmores, who founded the Unity movement, were students of Mrs. Hopkins, and the founders of both the Religious Science and Divine Science movements were greatly influenced by her teachings, too. Dr. H. B. Jeffery, who was reportedly a student of hers, also wrote succinctly of this prayer method in his book, *Mystical Teachings*.[2]

The Holy Bible also contains numerous passages for invoking angel-powers in times of need. Abraham promised: "Jehovah before whom I walk will send his angel with thee, and prosper thy ways." (Genesis 24:40)

---

1. See her books, *Scientific Christian Mental Practice* and *High Mysticism*, both published by DeVorss & Co., Marina del Rey, CA 90294.

2. Jeffery, *Mystical Teachings* (Christ Truth League, Fort Worth, TX, 1954)

WHEN OTHER PRAYER METHODS
HAVE NOT WORKED

All religions and cultures have taught that a man's word is his power. Many teachings have realized the special power of written words. The Chinese had such an affection for the written word that they have taught for centuries never to tear up a sheet of writing, nor to misuse any paper with written words on it, even if it has no further practical use. The Greeks have long believed that words are filled with cosmic power; that one can do anything with words, build or destroy.

A Prayer Method That Worked for a Businessman in Germany: Since I began steadfastly using the angel-writing method of prayer described in *The Prospering Power of Love*, my life has improved in amazing ways.

When I began using this special prayer method, first changes came *within* me, and later, changes began to come in the circumstances of my life. This is especialy gratifying since other prayer methods had not worked for me.

PROSPEROUS RESULTS

He Went from Rags to Riches in Europe: Even though I am a professional person, I was living in one room, barely surviving financially. Then I read about the angel-writing method in *The Prospering Power of Love.*

I began to write to my Prosperity Angel, asking its help. Within two years I literally went from "rags to riches." Increased supply came miraculously through my work, and in other ways. *Within three years from the time I began writing to my Prosperity Angel, I was able to retire!*

I now travel worldwide, visiting the great religious shrines, engaging in charity work, and helping others. Truly my Prosperity Angel has become my best friend. I still write to him often and ask his help, both for myself and others. I have also found it powerful to write to the Prosperity Angel of other people, inviting their own angel to aid them.

How Abundance Came to Her in Arizona: A short while ago I read of how a divorced mother felt she should take her children and move from California to Idaho. Her former husband said if she did he would give her no more child support money. She wrote to his angel and he *did* continue to support their children anyway.

I had a long-standing debt from my former husband for child support he owed us. In reading the above story, I decided to try it. I wrote to my former husband's angel and asked him for help.

Two days later I called him and proposed a solution of how he could help me out financially. He gave me more money than I had ever dreamed he would! He was nicer and more agreeable to me than he had ever been. Thanks for enlightening my mind to this mystical yet practical prayer method. *I now use the angel-writing method to solve all kinds of problems.*

Better Job in Wisconsin: A businesswoman was dissatisfied with her job, so she began to write to the angel of her boss, and of her job. Three days later her boss fired her, and she pronounced it good. A week later she had a far better job, more pay, and happier working conditions.

How He Collected Money in Nevada: A realtor reported that he has collected thousands and thousands of dollars from people who would not previously pay him — once he began to write to their angels.

Stolen Property Returned in Texas: We had a brand new truck stolen out of our locked dealership. Instead of getting upset, I wrote to the angel of the person who had taken this truck, asking him to release it.

A few days later, we received a phone call saying the vehicle had been found abandoned, out of state, with the keys still in the ignition. Except for one dent in the fender, it is in good shape. Our insurance company is taking care of that, and having it returned to us. That was fast service — both in inner and outer ways!

In New York, a Minister's Prayer for Her Church Was Answered: Three days after I began writing to the prosperity angel of our church, asking its help, a gentleman came through the door of our sanctuary to invite me, a minister, to move my work into a temple he had just bought.

He had found some of our literature, liked it, and wanted that kind of church housed in his building. I praise God and our prosperity angel for this turn of events — since it frees me from all financial strain so that I can minister on the spiritual level where I am needed so much.

HEALING RESULTS

Healing in Illinois: The friend of a business-man in Chicago was hospitalized, not expected to live. When this businessman learned of his friend's condition, he wrote to the sick man's angel, asking its help in healing him. The next time he heard from the friend, he was not only out of the hospital, but back at work!

Healing of Alcoholism in California: About two years ago I wrote to my ex-husband's angel, asking its help in freeing him from the drinking habit that was ruining his life. It had already ruined our marriage. I asked his angel to help him make peace with our son, who still needed contact with him.

It seemed a big request to make, since my former husband had been an alcoholic since he was fourteen years old. Also at the time I wrote to his angel, my ex-husband had not communi-cated with me or our son for twelve years.

Nevertheless, two months ago he contacted our son, and we learned that he had stopped drinking just about the time I had written to his angel. My son now has a father he can be proud of, after so many years of having none. What a wonderfully effective prayer method the angel-writing technique is. I only wish people everywhere knew about it. What a different world this could be.

Lady in Virginia Loses Twenty Pounds: A couple of years ago I decided to write to my angel concerning a weight problem. I was very enthusiastic about it, and through that method, I lost twenty pounds.

Rehabilitation from Drugs for A Vietnam Veteran in New York: Since we began writing to his angel, my son has gone on a drug rehabilitation program and is doing fine. Considering the physical and mental condition he has been in since he returned from the war, this is a miracle. He has gone to work for the government — another miracle.

HAPPY RESULTS IN RELATIONSHIPS

Family Harmonized in Africa: I wrote to my wife's angel when she was filled with resentment and criticism. She has responded positively ever since. My son has become more harmonious, too, as a result of this special prayer method.

Hostility Dissolved in Illinois: The angel-writing prayer method really works. We had been trying to get help in paying our hospital bills, and the man we spoke to was very hostile. I wrote to his angel asking its help, and the next time I spoke to him he had completely changed. *I have also been busy writing daily to our own angels of prosperity, healing, love and marriage, and we are seeing notable improvement on all levels of our lives.*

Lawsuit Dropped in Texas: A businesswoman learned that a lawsuit was being filed against her, very unfairly. She had been a victim of circumstances in which someone else was responsible, yet she was being blamed for the mix-up and being sued. It was very frustrating until she remembered to write to the angel of the situation, asking that the legal matter be cleared up quickly and in peace. Things suddenly got very quiet after they had been most unpleasant. The quietness continued for several weeks. Then she learned that the lawsuit had been dropped.

A Memorable Mother's Day in Pennsylvania: The biggest piece of happiness which has come my way in a long time is that I got to spend Mother's Day with my son and daughter. Because of a previously bitter divorce action, to see them again seemed a miracle. We went to the movies in the afternoon, and spent a leisurely dinner together. My son gave me a book and a card signed "love." I now look at that card daily. He even leaned over the table and kissed me. My daughter gave me a potted plant.

We had a pleasant relaxed three-hour dinner together in a restaurant. It was such a happy time. I looked up the entry made in my diary on Mother's Day last year, and it was a barren, lonely day for me. This one was in direct contrast. It still makes me happy to think about it. I shall continue dwelling on "divine love" and writing to the angels of all concerned.

WRITE TO A SPECIFIC ANGEL TO MEET A SPECIFIC NEED

If writing to a person's angel in a general way does not seem to get results, sometimes it is more powerful to get specific, and to write to the angel of that person's particular need: such as writing to the Angel of Protection, the Angel of Healing, the Angel of Love and Marriage, the Angel of Harmony and Happiness, the Angel of Wisdom and Guidance, the Angel of Prosperity and Wealth, or the Angel of Spiritual Growth and Understanding.

THE ANGEL OF DIVINE PROTECTION

Before traveling or going forth into any challenging situation, it is wise to declare: "THE

ANGEL OF DIVINE PROTECTION GOES BEFORE ME, SHIELDING ME FROM ANY NEGATIVE EXPERIENCES" or "THE ANGEL OF DIVINE PROTECTION GOES BEFORE ME AND PREPARES MY WAY." The prophet Malachi might have been speaking of his angel-protector when he said, "Behold, I send my messenger, and he shall prepare the way before me" (Malachi 3:1).

Two missionaries were passing through a dangerous jungle region where robbers were waiting to attack them. But as the missionaries approached, they prayed for divine protection. The robbers saw a "third person," much larger than life-size, traveling with the missionaries and apparently guarding them. The presence of this third party, or Angel of Protection, both puzzled and frightened the robbers, so that the missionaries were saved from harm.

THE ANGEL OF HEALING

The Hebrews of old felt that Raphael was the Angel of Healing. At times you may wish to decree and/or write out: "ANGEL OF HEALING, COME FORTH HERE AND NOW."

A story appeared in the newspapers in England many years ago about a woman who had been ill for five years and was dying from advanced tuberculosis. Doctors had long despaired of saving her, and relatives had gathered round as she stopped breathing and appeared to be gone. Minutes later, she suddenly took a deep breath and roused as she said conversationally, "Yes, I am listening. Who is it?" At that moment those in the room saw an angel bending over her sickbed and replying, "Your sufferings are over. Get up and walk."

When she asked for her robe, it caused a great commotion, because she had been bedridden for months. She then walked into another room and asked for food, though she had not had a solid meal for months.

After five years of intense suffering, she quickly regained her health, and medical tests revealed there was not a trace of the disease left in her body. Thereafter, she ate well, slept well, and was quite calm and peaceful. Nothing seemed to tire or excite her. The angel had told her that her life was being spared so that she might help to heal others. So she spent a great deal of time in intercessory prayer for the sick in her village, asking the Angel of Healing to make them whole. Her life took on new meaning and satisfaction as many healings occurred.

THE ANGEL OF PROSPERITY

Once when I was planning a six weeks' lecture trip, I decided to test the angel prayer method by asking that the Angel of Prosperity go before me making prosperous and successful my way. When lecturing for business, professional or convention groups, a professional lecture fee was often in order. But the offerings received when lecturing in churches were sometimes so small they did not pay one's expenses—and this was to be a lecture trip for churches.

However, on this trip, after sending the Angel of Prosperity before me, something happened that had never happened before: Along the way people kept privately saying, "I have read your books and have been helped by them. I want to show my appreciation by sharing a special tithe offering with you." The result was that I went home carrying a number of tithe checks as special gifts to me personally. They helped to defray costs I had so often had to meet on my own.

THE ANGEL OF WEALTH

A businessman recently wrote: "I came out of financial limitation and despair by writing to my Prosperity Angel daily. But then I kept waiting to go further: from general prosperity to definite wealth. That did not happen until I got more specific and began to write to the Angel of Wealth. Now, at last, I am financially independent."

THE ANGEL OF RELEASE

If you have been unable to gain release from health, financial, human relations or other types of problems, writing to the Angel of Freedom and Release can be very effective, too. Once when I had been unable to gain freedom from some people who I felt were using me in a number of ways, I began writing to the Angel of Release, asking its help. I was soon shown how to claim my freedom so that I was able to gain complete release from them. This new-found freedom soon proved to be a blessing to all concerned. "The good of one was the good of all."

Special Note: For a free copy of the author's "How to Write to the Angel" outline, please write her.

A SPECIAL METHOD OF LOVE—

Part II

— Chapter 6 —

John, in his Revelation, speaks of writing to the angels of the seven churches. (Revelation 1:19, 20) The word "church" most often symbolizes spiritual consciousness. The seven churches are symbolic of the seven types of people whom we can best reach spiritually by writing to their angels or higher selves in specific ways. These may be people we have seemed unable to reach in other ways—either through our general prayers for them, or by writing to their angels of healing, prosperity, love, wealth, release, as described in the previous chapter.

FIRST: HOW TO REACH THE
EXCITABLE TYPE

*"To the angel of the church in Ephesus
write."* (Revelation 2:1)

The word "Ephesus" means "desirable, appealing." You may know appealing people who are
hard to reach. Their outward life is full of ex-
citement. They are emotional, lovers of amuse-
ment, theatrical in their tastes, dramatic in
everything they do. Paul spent three years preach-
ing Truth in Ephesus, because he realized such
people were hard to reach and help.

The wonderful thing to remember about those
whom you are trying to help in this category is
that they have an intense desire for greater good
in their lives. Though they seem unsettled, they
are easy to know, pleasant and agreeable, and
they are interested in the finer things of life. By
writing to their angels, stating the Truth about
them, you easily reach that deeper phase of their
nature, and they happily respond.

I once knew a fine person of this type. He was
an emotional man with an exciting life and a
flair for the dramatic. He owed me for some work
I had done for his firm. Several months had
passed and I had not been paid. My affirmations
had brought no results.

Finally I remembered the angel-writing technique, and one night (quite late) I quietly wrote "TO THE ANGEL OF (let us say) JOHN BROWN, I BLESS YOU AND GIVE THANKS THAT YOU ARE HANDLING THIS FINANCIAL MATTTER PROMPTLY, AND THAT I AM IMMEDIATELY AND COMPLETELY PAID." (I wrote this statement fifteen times, because many mystics believed that fifteen is the number that dissolves adversity and hard conditions.)

After writing out the statement, I felt much better about the situation and was able to release it completely from my mind. Two days later, my friend telephoned to say that I would receive it by mail the following day — and I did!

SECOND: HOW TO REACH
THE BITTER-SWEET TYPE

"And to the angel of the church in Smyrna write." (Revelation 2:8)

The word "Smyrna" means "flowing substance." Smyrnians make a fine appearance. They are lovers of show, beauty, adornment. They live beyond their means and usually have financial problems.

A businessman was having great difficulty with his wife, who had divorced him. He was heartbroken because he still loved her. He had tried to talk with her about reconciliation, but she was very confused, and he could not reason with her.

He learned of this special method of love and was fascinated with the idea, realizing that his wife was this second type. She was an attractive lady, and loved fine things. In fact, that had been one of their basic problems: her tastes had been much too expensive for his pocketbook.

He began writing each night to her angel, asking help in straightening out their marriage. One day, after he had not heard from her for some time, she contacted him, tearfully declaring that their divorce had been a mistake. Soon they were remarried. This man has found it possible to maintain peace and harmony with his wife by continuing to write to her angel.

THIRD: HOW TO REACH THE ALOOF INTELLECTUAL TYPE

"And to the angel of the church in Pergamum write." (Revelation 2:12)

The word "Pergamum" means "strongly united, closely knit." This is the grand, often wealthy, aristocratic type—literary, scientific, artistic, lovers of society and statescraft, strongly united, closely knit in family, social, and business relationships. These persons may be suspicious of strangers, new friends, new ideas.

A young man fell in love and wanted to marry. But the girl of his choice was from a close-knit family that did not want to release her emotionally. This family group was suspicious of new people, new ways of doing things, all new ideas. In fact, they were strongly united against the invasion of anything new in their lives.

The young man realized that from a human standpoint, it seemed hopeless to try to win the girl, even though she was in love with him, because of her strong family ties. Being a Truth student, he reasoned that the only possible way to deal with the possessiveness of her family was through the practice of love.

It was at this point that he learned of love's special method. He wrote to the girl's angel and to the angel of her family, decreeing for her emotional freedom, a happy marriage, and a family divinely adjusted to this change. For some months, he continued this angel-writing technique, with no visible results. Then suddenly everything changed. He could sense a freedom that had not previously existed. He proposed, and they were soon married. Though it took her family some time to adjust to the change and to accept him emotionally into the family, they finally did so wholeheartedly.

FOURTH: HOW TO REACH THE ZEALOUS, QUARRELSOME TYPE

*"And to the angel of the church of Thya-
tira write."* (Revelation 2:18)

"Thyatira" means "rushing headlong, frantic, zealous, quarrelsome, easily offended." People of this type have greater ideas than inner ability for producing idealistic results. Thyatirans are quite often interested in athletics.

A housewife learned that the instructor at a health club was being harsh with the teenage boys he was instructing. Though her son and his friends were upset by this harsh treatment, they did not wish her to interfere, feeling that would bring only more scorn from their instructor. The mother asked the boys to begin writing to the angel of their instructor, decreeing fair treatment and understanding. She joined them in their angel-writing project.

For a time no results were apparent. Suddenly, however, the instructor announced he was leaving his job to take a better position with a local college. Along with an increased income, the new job would allow him time to work on his master's degree, which had long been his desire. The mother then realized that the young instructor's harsh treatment apparently had stemmed from his own frustration and job dissatisfaction. The amazing result was that this woman's son later won a trophy from the health club—a trophy topped with the figure of an angel!

FIFTH: HOW TO REACH THE
FEARFUL BODY DEVOTEES

*"And to the angel of the church
in Sardis write."* (Revelation 3:1)

The word "Sardis" means "prince of power, timid, apprehensive, always fearful about something." These people are body devotees. They are afraid of drafts, accidents, what they eat. They are always seeking the comfortable, soft, pleasant things of bodily life. No books, lessons, or instructions seem to quench their fears, but writing to their angels uplifts the bold, brave, dauntless spirit in them, and they become "princes of power."

This type of person is always changing his mind. The throat, which is the power center in the body, is usually a weak spot. He may develop a sore throat or some other throat ailment when he becomes fearful.

Such a person has great potential for becoming a powerful individual. You awaken that power center within him and bring it alive through writing to his angel. This gives him a stability and fearlessness that he desires to express.

A man was once having difficulty trying to bring a business matter to a conclusion. It had been pending for a long time. Everyone involved was congenial and wished to conclude negotiations except one man, who kept changing his mind. He seemed unsure about every aspect of the matter.

The businessman heard of the angel-writing method and realized that the man who kept changing his mind was timid, apprehensive, fearful, unsure. He wrote to the man's angel, asking that the business matter be brought to an early, appropriate conclusion, so that all involved would be satisfied and blessed.

A few days later, the man who had stalled for a long time said, "Come down to my office tomorrow morning and the papers will be ready to sign." Then he added, as though it were his idea, "This situation has been delayed long enough, and I am anxious to conclude it."

SIXTH: HOW TO REACH THE LOVING-WORKS TYPE

"And to the angel of the church in Philadelphia write." (Revelation 3:7)

The word "Philadelphia" means "brotherly love, fraternal love, universal love." People of this type talk much about the brotherhood of man, but love to them means outer works alone, rather than an inner consciousness of love. These are the philanthropists of human existence. Community organizations, clubs, fraternal groups, civic groups, churches are all filled with people seeking brotherly love, universal love. They sometimes become frustrated through exhausting themselves in loving works.

If you find yourself in a group or organization where the loving works do not seem to be balanced by an inner consciousness of love, you can write to the angel of that organization, asking that divine love come alive in the thoughts as well as in the actions of the group. As you do, those people who are not in tune with divine love will fade harmoniously out of the group, and those who are lovingly in tune with its aims and purposes will appear. In this secret, quiet way both inner and outer harmony can be established and maintained.

An executive found himself in the midst of organizational disharmony. He was not sure just who was responsible for the unrest and critical attitudes found in the group. He tried various methods for reestablishing harmony, but the group remained aloof, critical, inharmonious.

In desperation, he began writing daily to the angel of that organization, asking for help in reestablishing a consciousness of love. Then he wrote: "I CAST THIS BURDEN ON THE ANGEL OF

DIVINE LOVE. THE ANGEL OF LOVE NOW COMES
ALIVE IN THIS SITUATION AND IN ALL PERSONS CON-
NECTED WITH THIS ORGANIZATION. THE ANGEL OF
DIVINE LOVE NOW REIGNS SUPREME."

Soon several volunteer workers resigned their
jobs, leaving the organization, and new workers
appeared who were eager to contribute to the
progress of the organization in a harmonious
way. Peace and progress were established and
maintained.

SEVENTH: HOW TO REACH THE
UNSTABLE WANDERERS

*"And to the angel of the church
in Laodicea write."* (Revelation 3:14)

The word "Laodicea" means "justice and
judgment." People of this type often have an
injustice complex. They are unstable, unsettled, changeable, wanderers seeking new doc-
trines and new places. They often change their
religious beliefs and their political views. They
are restless, critical. They usually feel that they
have been wronged or misused.

You find this type of person going from one
job to another, from one church to another,
from one club to another. They are the "join-
ers" who do not remain with anything long

enough to discover whether it will benefit them or not.

When you write to the angel of such a person, decree that the divine law of love and justice is doing its perfect work in his life and affairs, and that he is being divinely guided into his right place. He will subconsciously respond more and more to your high vision of rightness and stability for him.

WRITE TO YOUR OWN ANGEL

In writing to another's angel, it may appear that nothing is being accomplished. Then, suddenly, everything will shift, changes will come, and matters that had seemed destined for failure will clear up very quickly; but sometimes one must practice patience before this happens.

The word *angel* means "messenger of God." Do not fail to write to your own angel when it seems that your life is filled with defeat, or when you are tempted to criticize and condemn yourself. *The Metaphysical Bible Dictionary*[1] explains: "The office of the angels is to guard and guide and direct the natural forces of mind

---

1. Published by Unity School of Christianity, Unity Village, MO 64065 (1931).

and body, which have in them the future of the whole man."

Emma Curtis Hopkins writes:

> "The Angel of His Presence accompanies every man. . . . This high leadership is every man's heritage. He need not fear dangerous days or vicious circumstances while he is aware that his angel goes before him, pleads his cause and defends him."[2]

When challenges arise, say to yourself: "I HAVE NOTHING TO FEAR. MY GUARDIAN ANGEL GOES BEFORE ME, MAKING RIGHT MY WAY." Decree it for others. A businesswoman was concerned about having to make an out-of-town buying trip, which required that she drive two hundred miles in rain and fog, accompanied by her ailing husband, whom she could not leave at home alone. A friend said, "You have nothing to fear, because your guardian angel will be with you."

Upon returning from the buying trip, she said to her friend: "It *did* seem that we were accompanied by an angel. As I drove out of town, within a few minutes the sky cleared of fog, the rain stopped, and the sun shone through. There was no more bad weather on the entire trip. The drive helped my husband's

2. Hopkins, *High Mysticism* (Marina del Rey, CA, Devorss & Co.)

spirits and he suffered no ill effects from it. Financially, this proved to be the most profitable buying trip I have made in a long time."

ANGEL-WRITING PRODUCES
NEITHER HURT NOR HARM

Never expect your angel or that of another to honor any requests that might hurt or harm. Be willing that something infinitely better than that which you tentatively want will come as you use love's special method. This will open the way for your good and for the good of all involved to manifest in an unlimited, satisfying manner.

For invoking love's special method, meditate often upon the promise of the Psalmist:

> No evil shall befall you. No scourge come near your tent. For he will give his angels charge of you, to guard you in all your ways.

> (Psalms 91:10, 11)

HOW LOVE PROSPERS

— Chapter 7 —

I must admit that the first time I read these words written by Charles Fillmore in his book *Prosperity*,[1] I was skeptical about their practical value:

> Tell me what kind of thoughts you are hold-
> ing about yourself and your neighbors and I
> can tell you just what you may expect in the
> way of health, finances, and harmony. . . .
> You cannot love and trust in God if you hate
> and distrust men. The two ideas, love and
> hate, or trust and mistrust, simply cannot both
> be present in your mind at one time, and when

---

1. Published by Unity School of Christianity, Unity Village, MO 64065, p.118.

you are entertaining one, you may be sure the other is absent. Trust other people and use the power that you accumulate from that act to trust God. There is magic in it: it works wonders; love and trust are dynamic, vital powers.

These words are to be found in the chapter on indebtedness. I could not imagine love having anything to do with debt!

LOVE DISSOLVES DEBT
FOR A BUSINESSMAN

But love *does* have something to do with the dissolution of indebtedness. The owner of a furniture company in Alabama once related one of his many experiences along this line:

This man had a customer who refused to pay for a washing machine purchased from his store. The finance company finally reclaimed it; then the customer came rushing into the furniture store and started screaming at the proprietor in vile language. This raging man weighed nearly two hundred and forty pounds, and he stood about six feet, three inches tall, whereas the store owner is a much smaller man. As the customer made his abusive accusations, the furniture dealer listened quietly; and whenever possible, he declared between accusations,

"But [naming the man], I love you!" He made this statement dozens of times until finally the enraged customer left in utter disgust.

In about thirty minutes, he returned to apologize for his behavior, and to thank the furniture-store owner for the way he had dealt with the situation. The customer then explained that he had lost his last job because of his temper, which had caused him to assault a man who later had to be hospitalized.

He further stated that the way the dealer had handled the situation had turned the tide of his temper and made him see how foolish he had been. He promised that as soon as he found another job he would pay for the washing machine—and he did. He became a fine, stable customer of this dealer, who says now that it was not easy to say to another man, especially a raging one, "I love you," but that he had found it well worth the effort.

LAWYER USES LOVE TO COLLECT MONEY

A lawyer, who had also studied Charles Fillmore's book *Prosperity*, once related that he collected two big accounts by releasing love and trust as dynamic, vital powers.

At the end of the year, in going over his books, he found two especially large accounts still due. He recalled that Mr. Fillmore had written, "A thought of debt will produce debt." He reasoned that as long as he believed in debt, resented debt, or attached the thought of debt to himself or others, he would remain in debt. So, to overcome such negative thoughts, and also to invoke the power of love and trust, the lawyer made a mental note of the clients who owed him large amounts. He began blessing their names daily, each one separately, and sincerely erasing the idea of debt attached to each one.

After he had been using this system for a short time, the two clients who owed the largest sums settled with him on the same day, one of them mailing his check for the full amount from a distant state.

HOW THEY USED LOVE TO PROSPER

I no longer doubt Charles Fillmore's claims on the power of love to prosper one's self and others. I have discovered that it is true: Love and trust *are* dynamic, vital powers which seem to contain magic powers that can work wonders in your life. The following are but a few of the reports I have received from readers of mine over the years which surely indicate this:

First Vacation in Eight Years in Ohio: I had not had a vacation in eight years when I began to declare, "DIVINE LOVE FORESEES EVERYTHING AND RICHLY PROVIDES EVERYTHING NOW."

A friend soon presented me the gift of a round-trip ticket to Florida. Another friend invited me to share her hotel accommodations while she was there on a business trip. The only cost I had was my meals. This vacation was such a blessing to me.

Better Living Arrangements in California: After I began to daily use "divine love" statements, miracles happened. A friend soon invited me to move into her home, and use her spare bedroom. Our sharing of expenses has cut them in half. I sold most of my old furniture in just four days—another miracle. The income from this sale has helped tide me over until some income that was pending is released. "The prospering power of love" has worked for me!

How He Passed Realtor's Exam in Massachusetts: I took a most difficult and tricky real estate examination. This particular test, designed to eliminate the maximum number of candidates, also required memorizing one hundred and fifty pages of legal data.

I dislike reading textbooks and my eyes glazed over whenever I tried to study for the exam. Furthermore, I had not taken any exam for forty years, and never one of this type—which required so much memory and accuracy. But I remembered reading that a person should pour love into whatever he does. I did, and I passed!

Cabinet Shop Prospers in New York: Since we began to use "divine love" statements, work has poured into our cabinet shop. We got so busy that we had to hire another employee, who is very helpful. Love *is* prospering us.

A Single Parent Prospered in the West Indies: Since first studying *The Prospering Power of Love*, I have often used Divine Love affirmations to help me meet my needs, and the good has always come — sometimes in miraculous ways.

I did not have a cent, yet with the help of divine love, I was able to purchase a $4000 car. My children and I had long needed a car, but as a single parent I had felt we should not attempt it. After food, clothes and rent, there was little left. I had no savings except what I gave to God's work in tithes. I called this my "spiritual bank."

When my cousin said she was getting a new car, I asked her to consider holding her old one for me. At home the children and I began to declare: "DIVINE LOVE NOW PROVIDES US WITH THE MONEY TO BUY THE PERFECT CAR FOR US, AND TO PAY FOR IT WITHOUT STRAIN."

I was then able to borrow $500 from a small insurance policy and $500 from a friend. But the bank would not accept this amount because, for a used car, they required one-half in cash. My cousin said she would hold the car for me, although she had several cash offers on it.

The children agreed with me that "DIVINE LOVE IS IN CHARGE AND THE BEST WILL HAPPEN." In spite of my disappointment, I was able to release the matter to divine love. When I did, my cousin delivered the car to me, and said I could begin making payments when my loan arrangements had been satisfactorily worked out. So we had the car in time for summer holidays.

Divine love came through for us. At work I soon got a new salary agreement with back pay of $2500, and a raise of $350 per month. So I was able to make the down payment and monthly car payments without strain, as we had affirmed. It is such a joy to prosper with the help of divine love.

Love Cuts Prices in California: It's true that plants respond to love. For weeks, I had admired a certain potted plant at the supermarket, but the price did not fit into my budget. Yet I thought of that plant often with much affection.

Last Saturday as I shopped, I again looked at that plant, thinking how much I would like to have it in my home. Just as I was turning away, a clerk walked by and said, "We're reducing the plants on this shelf to ninety-nine cents today." Zap. Love cuts prices!

DIVINE LOVE CAN MEET EVERY NEED

A long time friend has often said, "Divine love always has and always will meet every need." Yes, it will, when we give it our attention.

Love to the Rescue in Michigan: I was on the way home after teaching a class sixty miles away. There was snow on the side of the road, but I was not aware of ice on the road. It was 1:00 A.M. and I was whizzing along when suddenly the car landed in a snowbank up to the floor of the car, and up to my knees when I got out of the car.

I started walking up the road in the dark declaring, "I CALL FORTH DIVINE LOVE TO PERFOM ANY MIRACLE NEEDED IN THIS SITUATION NOW." Within—not minutes, but moments—a man arrived in a van. He had a CB radio, a four-wheel drive, a chain and the "know how" to get my car out of that snowbank. Within fifteen minutes from the time I skidded, I was on my way home. The only damage to my car was a dented left door.

When I had called forth divine love to work a miracle for me at 1:00 A.M. in the dark in a snowbank, it did! This was a magnificent experience for me in the wonder-working power of love.

He Meets Prison Experience Victoriously in Pennsylvania: I have been granted commutation of my life sentence. The board followed the recommendation of the institution staff that I should serve five more years before being considered for parole.

I was disappointed with this decision, but not discouraged. I shall continue my relationship with God, and do the best I can to compensate for my regrettable crime. I shall continue to use prayer statements on divine love from *The Prospering Power of Love* in order to meet my prison experiences victoriously.

Divine Love Helps Her to Relocate in America: "Divine love" affirmations have worked miracles in my life. Although I am new in this country, I already have a flock of friends and even a prayer partner.

How She Got Married and Stayed Married in Oregon: I decided last year I was not going to let this good way of thinking and living pass me by. I wanted to get married and got very specific on my prayer list about the qualities I desired in a husband. I used "divine love" statements daily.

We met in June and were married in January. I have never been happier in my whole life. This marriage is the best thing that could have happened to me. When there have been adjustments to make in our marriage, I have used "divine love" affirmations and have studied *The Prospering Power of Love*. Any difficulties have always disappeared. *Divine love has worked a miracle in my life, and I am convinced it can do the same for anyone else who will call on it!*

Love Was Soul-Stretching in North Carolina: Divine love works in mysterious ways. I took the best from two adverse marriages. "The best" was two fine children that came through challenging experiences which seemed insurmountable at the time. Through those "soul-

stretching" espisodes, there has come great
spiritual growth within me. I feel there is
emerging a more purified and refined nature.
My children are doing well in high school and
college, and I am now active in a study group
which I find inspiring.

LOVE IS RELEASED THROUGH THE
PROSPERING TENTH

Several decades ago, when I came into the
ministry out of the business world, a lovely lady
minister with whom I worked briefly asked me
to help with her correspondence. When she saw
some of the letters I had prepared she said,
"These are fine, but put some love into them."
In answering her mail I had observed the letter
of the law, but had overlooked including the
spirit of love.

*Putting God first financially on a regular,
consistent basis is a sure way to release the
prospering power of love—provided you deliberately put love into your acts of giving. Be sure
to tithe with love.* People sometimes tithe to
observe the letter of the law, but do not reap its
full benefits when they have not done so in a
spirit of love.[2]

2. Chapters on tithing may be found in the following
books by the author: *The Prosperity Secret of the Ages,*

It is easy to put love into your giving when you realize that the first tenth of all you receive belongs to God anyway; and that you are merely returning to Him the sacred tenth of all He has and is giving to you. "The tenth is holy unto Jehovah." (Leviticus 27:32)

This realization takes the fear and resentment out of giving. Instead, it puts love of God, and appreciation for His many blessings, into your acts of sharing. "Thou shalt remember Jehovah thy God, for it is He that giveth thee power to get wealth." (Deuteronomy 8:18)

THE SECRET OF FINANCIAL INCREASE

The word "tithe" means "tenth." Since ancient times "ten" has been considered the magic number of increase. All great civilizations and cultures have taught and practiced the tithing law of prosperity. They have felt that by returning a tenth of all they received to their creator, they would become attuned to the wisdom and wealth of the universe. Tithing, as an act of spiritual worship, and as an act for invoking

The Dynamic Laws of Healing, Dare to Prosper, The Prospering Power of Prayer, Open Your Mind to Prosperity, Open Your Mind to Receive, The Secret of Unlimited Prosperity, The Millionaires of Genesis, The Millionaire Moses, The Millionaire Joshua and *The Millionaire from Nazareth.*

universal abundance, has been practiced since the time of primitive man.

As the Hebrews of old proved, to tithe is to prosper. In more recent times, John D. Rockefeller's total tithes for the year of 1855 were $9.50. By 1934 his tithes had grown to a total of $531 million dollars. He often commented, "God gave me my wealth."

Sharing is the beginning of financial increase, as pointed out by the prophet:

> Bring ye the whole tithe into the storehouse, that there may be food in my house, and prove me now herewith saith Jehovah of hosts, if I will not open you the windows of heaven, and pour you out a blessing, that there shall not be room enough to receive it.
>
> (Malachi 3:10)

As time goes by, the faithful tither will find himself remarkably blessed, just as Malachi promised. In fact, those who have followed his advice on a regular basis, practicing systematic tithing, have usually found that the time came when they had more to "share and to spare" than they had previously dreamed possible!

THE COUNTLESS BLESSINGS OF TITHING

Of all of life's universal laws that I have written about over the years, the tithing law of prosperity seems to be the one that most fascinates people, probably because it carries with it an ancient heritage of success. I receive more mail on the subject of tithing than on all the other prosperity laws combined!

Here are just a few reports of the countless blessings that the practice of tithing has brought:

Anxiety About Money is Gone in California: At first I resented the subject of tithing. But I soon realized that any prosperity law that had made millionaires of the Hebrews of old, and so many people since, was worth trying.

When I began to tithe, all the anxiety about financial matters that had been with me so long left! I have felt guided, protected, safer, calmer. *More than any other single prosperity technique, tithing has changed my life.*

A Loser Became a Winner in Texas: I now have a new rock home in one of the most beautiful neighborhoods of our city. I recently bought a lake lot on which to build a vacation house. I now own my own office building, and my practice is doing well. Tithing has turned this former loser into a winner.

Income Tripled in Less Than a Year in Missouri: Looking at my financial records has reminded me that my income has tripled in less than one year, since I began tithing! The act of giving makes me feel so rich.

How He Avoided Problems in New York: I feel sorry for those people who are too indif-

ferent to tithing so that they hold on tightly to
every cent. The result is that they find themselves in unpleasant situations, spending far
more money than the tithe in an effort to get
freed of annoying, unwanted experiences —
which they would not have had in the first
place had they put God first financially. To
tithe is the easier way to succeed, and I give
thanks I found it.

**Why Her Tithing Was Not Productive in Illi-
nois:** I tithed in the past, but felt I wasn't supposed to expect anything in return (even
though the Bible clearly said I *should*) — so, of
course, I did not receive the blessings due me.
And I stopped tithing in 1973.

I feel much happier now that I know it is
normal and right to expect the Biblical prosperity promises about tithing to be fulfilled for
me. It suddenly becomes a joy to give. After
studying the tithing law of prosperity further,
it has become clear to me why I had those accidents, and all those aches and pains. Since
pledging with God to pay my tithes regularly,
the pain has diminished, and my future looks
bright.

A Widow Prospers in Pennsylvania: I have
been widowed for eight years. I live in my own
home, and I receive $260 per month Social Se-
curity. But I gladly share my tithes. I have begun to give in every way that is revealed to me
in order to make room to receive more. It
works! A lovely trip came to me from my son
and his wife. We drove through the state of
Virginia this fall. Now my granddaughter has
arranged for me to fly to New Mexico to spend

a month, with relatives coming to visit from Arizona and Montana.

A Divorcee Makes a New Start in Nevada: Shortly after my divorce, my parents introduced me to *The Prospering Power of Love*. But I was not yet ready to accept the peace and prosperity that were mine to claim. Tithing was one part of Dr. Ponder's teachings that I had difficulty accepting. Instead, I continued in a state of financial struggle and fruitless mental effort.

Finally, when I had only $25 left and did not know where the next cent was coming from with which to provide for my children, I decided to tithe. I realized that putting God first financially was something I must do if I wished to prosper and succeed in life on a permanent and stable basis. The next day I received $190 which was a bonus from the company I left three months previously. I feel that I shall now go forward into a far more prosperous life than I have ever known. This is my spiritual heritage and I am claiming it.

Changing Where She Gave Her Tithe Brought Results in Arizona: I found myself resentful of giving to a congregation with which I no longer had a spiritual affinity, and which I had outgrown. I now give to the church where I get my spiritual help and inspiration, and I have prospered accordingly.

A FINAL WAY FOR INVOKING THE
PROSPERING POWER OF LOVE

May the foregoing experiences of others inspire you to invoke the prospering power of love
through putting God first financially—thereby
opening the way for the increase of abundant,
permanent good in every phase of your life. As
Malachi pointed out, you deserve nothing less!

See A SPECIAL NOTE FROM THE AUTHOR, next page.

A SPECIAL NOTE FROM THE AUTHOR

Through the generous outpouring of their tithes over the years, the readers of my books have helped me to financially establish three new churches—the most recent being a global ministry, the nondenominational *Unity Church Worldwide*, with headquarters in Palm Desert, California. Many thanks for your help in the past, and for all that you continue to share.

You are also invited to share your tithes with the churches of your choice—especially those which teach the truths stressed in this book. Such churches would include the metaphysical churches of Unity, Religious Science, Divine Science, Science of Mind, and other related churches, many of which are members of The International New Thought Movement. (For a list of such churches write The International New Thought Alliance, 7314 E. Stetson Drive, Scottsdale, Arizona 85251.) Your support of such churches can help spread the prosperous Truth that mankind is now seeking in this New Age of metaphysical enlightenment.